Searching for
Jonah

Searching for Jonah

Clues in Hebrew
and Assyrian History

Don E. Jones

LaPuerta Books and Media
www.lapuerta.tv
Santa Monica, California

ISBN: 978-0-9856227-1-8

Library of Congress Control Number: 2012914235

Cover art: *Jonah and the Whale,* acrylic on canvas (2004) by Keith A. Tucker www.KeithTuckerArt.com. Used with the kind permission of the artist.

Maps in the Appendix were redrawn from the author's original sketches.

Please send notifications of errata to the publisher at the e-mail address below, and we will correct future printings.

La Puerta

LaPuerta Books and Media
an imprint of La Puerta Productions, Santa Monica, CA USA 90405
info@lapuerta.tv

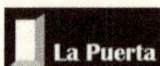

for Kathleen

Table of Contents

Introduction

Whatever its original form and composition, most scholars now hold that the *Book of Jonah* was set down in writing in the post-exilic period, no earlier than 450 BCE. The evidence is mostly internal, principally in the presence of Aramaic phraseology that cannot be earlier. The song of the prophet from the fish's belly (Jonah 2:1ff) may be as late as the Maccabean period (c. 175 BCE).[1] The latest limit is set by the external evidence of the Qumran (Dead Sea) Scrolls. The book was canonical and part of the *Book of the Twelve Prophets* in scrolls dated as early as 150 BCE. There are no major differences with familiar versions. The reign of Jeroboam II, associated with Jonah in II Kings 14:25, can be assigned as 735-745 with little probable error. The allusion does not insist that Jeroboam and Jonah be contemporary, so a case can be made for a historical Jonah as early as 900 BCE. Present knowledge does not permit bridging the gap between the eighth and the fifth centuries with certainty.[2] One of the purposes of this book is to develop this chronology more fully.

The story of Jonah must have originally been oral history, although we cannot rule out the possibility of a primitive version written by the prophet himself. By the very circumstance there was no dearth of witnesses — and Jonah showed no reluctance to tell of his affairs. Members of Israel's royal court, Jonah's fellow prophets, the sailors, and the multitude at Nineveh could not resist repeating a tale that has fascinated people in every age since. During Israel's Assyrian exile there was ample opportunity for cross-fertilization of these many first-person accounts. The symbolism that entered the early redactions should not be permitted to obscure the clues to a historical Jonah.

The Hebrew Exile, or more properly the *assimilation*, was an intimate contact of two widely different societies. Jonah's revelation of a God

---

[1] Paul Haupt, *American Philosophical Society Proceedings*, XLVI, 46 (Philadelphia: 1907): 151.

[2] The reader should bear in mind that the author's references to current time, the present, and modern events all date to about 1975.

intensely involved in both cultures was an ameliorating force that commanded attention and invited escalation to the moral and generalized level. Certainly early Talmudic references to Jonah are meant to emphasize God's care for Israel as a nation. As if the miracles of the canon were not sufficient, the glosses reach the level of incredibility. But they were not intended as history.

Somewhat more trustworthy are the various early Syriac versions. St. Ephraim the Syrian, Bishop of Edessa in 365 CE, had the advantage of acquaintance with the Mosul (Nineveh) area and its local traditions. His homilies gained wide acceptance in the Nestorian church, and he was declared a saint. Quotations from his prose poem "The Repentance of Nineveh" appear at the chapter openers of this book (translation by Rev. Henry Burgess, 1853).

Josephus, that stalwart Jewish historian of the first century, is almost apologetic about the miraculous incidents in *Jonah:* "Now I have given this account about him as I found it written (in our books)."[3] But Josephus does give valuable additional material about Jonah's contemporaries, presumably from written sources unavailable to us.

The early Christian fathers St. Jerome[4] and Pseudo-Epiphanius,[5] both about 400 CE, emphasize the philosophical content almost to the exclusion of the factual. They were more interested in purpose and ideas than in setting. *De Jona Oratio,* uncertainly attributed to Philo (c. 100), is of the same import.

Criticism remained on this level, vacillating according to the commentator's religious viewpoint, until relatively modern times. In passing we should mention the skepticism of Celsus (250 CE), Zosimus of Gaza (c. 500), and Tom Paine (1800). The tone of all is the same, though Paine was the sharpest: "The story of a whale swallowing Jonah, though a whale is large enough to do it, borders greatly on the

---

[3] Flavius Josephus, *Antiquities,* IX, 10:2 in William Whiston (tr.), *The Works of Flavius Josephus* (Cincinnati: 1841): 199.
[4] [tr. of Latin form] St. Jerome, *Commentary on Jonas.*
[5] Pseudo-Epiphanius [author uncertain], *De Vitis Prophetarium.*

marvelous; but it would have approached nearer to the idea of miracle if Jonah had swallowed the whale."[6]

The spade of the archaeologist has constructed the only platform for reasonable discussion of such divergent views. The excavations at Nineveh, commenced by P. E. Botta in 1843 and continued with such vigor by Sir A.H. Layard until 1894, rekindled the interest of theologians and scientists alike. Since that time the search for the historical Jonah can be based on more than conjecture.

Dr. Jacques Barzun reminds that "a large subject is like a mountain, which no beholder ever sees entire: if he climbs it he discovers only selected aspects; if he stands off, he sees but an outline and from one side only; if he flies over it, he flattens it out."[7] At the summits of religious experience, the lesson is often ignored or ridiculed — even slighted — by both friend and foe of the search for Deity.

This reluctance to establish several surveying stations has been particularly evident where the Holy Scriptures are concerned. But in recent generations, the same quest for knowledge that produced the skeptics is prompting a look from another direction. Such is the viewpoint of Dr. Nelson Glueck, who as an archaeologist trusts in "the amazing historical memory of the Bible."[8] Those Biblical phrases formerly dismissed as too obscure to understand or as patently false reveal exciting clues to cultural discovery on closer inspection. Thus do modern archaeology, linguistics, and physical science meet at a religious mountain of uncertain antiquity.

Perhaps no other part of the Bible illustrates this point more clearly than the *Book of Jonah*. The unseeing person is apt to lose historical perspective in the belly of the fish, and the visionary so often is blinded by the perceived light of pure faith. As the examples given previously show, the resulting dialogue has not been very productive of either knowledge or faith.

---

[6] Thomas Paine, *The Age of Reason* (New York: 1915): 64.
[7] Jacques Barzun and Henry Franklin Graff, *The Modern Researcher* (New York: 1957): 164.
[8] Nelson Glueck, *Rivers in the Desert* (New York: 1959): xi.

The author believes that the Bible is uniquely true in both moral and historical perspective. This faith places the search for allegory in a secondary position. It requires that clues to history must be traced and verified wherever possible. The historical sense then gives meaning and depth to the moral lessons. These incidents, in their important particulars, actually happened to a man. The spiritual value at once becomes more than a fable's maxim.

Now the great body of data available to us allows description of the Near East in the eighth century with some certainty. The conjecture enters when we try to relate the prophet to these events. The reader may hold back from some of the conclusions reached here. Even though stating the facts with some finality to permit the tale to be told entire, the author must agree that such linkages remain tentative. If fleshing out the character of Jonah adds to the reader's appreciation of his or her spiritual dilemma, then our purpose is achieved, and together we view the mountain from a fresh perspective.

A large subject is like a mountain, which no beholder ever sees entire: if he climbs it he discovers only selected aspects; if he stands off, he sees but an outline and from one side only; if he flies over it, he flattens it out.

- Jacques Barzun

1   What's in a Name?

The Idea of Name in Israel

> These boast in names alone,
> Because they are called children of the upright;
> It suffices them that they think
> They are named the sons of Jacob;
> By pious titles which they put on
> They foolishly believe they shall be justified.
> Their name is spread abroad through the world,
> with their sinful actions.
> They think they are righteous children,
> On account of (their father) Abraham,
> But that they have on them the name of Israel
> Is but the pride of words.
>   - "The Repentance of Nineveh," Part X, 142-154

Had Jonah been born into a Romance culture, his parents might have named him Columbus. Each of these seafarers entered history as "The Dove." Christopher Columbus, of course, inherited his surname. The Latin word *columbidae* now designates the entire pigeon family. The Hebrew equivalent *yownah* has passed from Western use except as a proper name. Across a score of centuries, the Genoese explorer was to be reminded more than once of his link with the Hebrew seafarer. When Columbus faced the stormy seas, he took heart from the example of Jonah's miraculous preservation. But more of that story later.

The meaning of Jonah's name is the single point of the Biblical account that has provoked little controversy. The Hebrew word transliterated *Jonah* occurs 50 times in the Old Testament. Whenever translated it becomes *dove* or *pigeon* — on that, there is no disagreement. The remaining instances refer to Jonah, son of Amittai, the prophet. So it is not surprising to find the statement in most commentaries that the prophet was named for a bird.

If this be so, what kind of bird is a *yownah?* The Old Testament Hebrew writers were careful to distinguish between the wild, migratory turtledove (designated *tor)* which wintered in Egypt and the rock dove or common pigeon, always nearby.[9] It is this latter specie (probably *Columba livia* or *Columba schimperi*) which may have been Jonah's natal omen.

Some scholars hear in the soft, moaning call of a dove the onomatopoetic source of its name — *yo-o-naah.* That call was familiar among the rocky cliffs of the Promised Land from Dan in the north, south to Beersheba. Even today in Galilee's Wadi Hammat (Pigeon Valley), the birds roost and nest by the thousands in fissures to be safe from preying hawks. There in the crannies, blue-gray plumage is good protective coloring, though the sheen of green and lilac neck feathers can betray.

But in the eighth century BCE, the life of a yownah held other perils. Moses had stipulated at Yahweh's command that either the turtledove or the rock dove could be used as a temple sacrifice (Leviticus 5:6-10). This provision was primarily for the poor farmer or the herdsman who might not own the animals he tended. The tor migrated away part of the year and the yownah alone was left to the fowler. So, by sling and snare, by net and throwing-stick, the birds were taken for sacrifice. Even small birds captured in the nest were acceptable. In fact the only safe place for a yownah was within the precincts of a holy place.

The dove is presented in the Bible as a symbol of gentleness, affection, humility, and even folly. But it had other connotations that were probably not unknown to the prophet's parents. The Canaanite use of the dove as a symbol of fertility is familiar to archaeologists. Statues, shrines, and figurines of the goddess Ishtar depict her suckling a dove and a serpent. Some etymologists trace the origin of the word *yownah* to a common root with another meaning "intoxicated passion." In their view the bird received such a name through its fecundity and the warmth of its mating habits. *Yayin yownah* (roughly, "lovey dovey")

---

[9] Although Palestine is host to immense flocks of migrating rock doves in spring and fall, many remain all winter.

would have been too attractive an alliteration to escape the attention of Jonah's young playmates.

But the primary Biblical imagery of the dove is one of peace. This is true in Hebrew history from Noah (Genesis 8:6) to the Messiah (Matthew 3:16-17). The judgment of Yahweh is past and reconciliation is complete. The dove returns with an olive branch in its beak.

This excursion into the meaning and use of the word *yownah* is necessary before attempting to answer the question: If Jonah was named by his parents, why did they choose such a strange name? St. Jerome gives a straightforward answer. It was because of the prophet's "complaining and mourning nature" — but whether this conclusion is based principally on Jerome's interpretation of the character of the adult Jonah is not clear.

The point is undeniable that the ancients had a far greater preoccupation with the idea of name than we do today. This goes much deeper than the simple difference in standards for choosing among personal names that a culture finds acceptable. The Sumerian creation epic, antedating both Hebrew and Babylonian versions, begins with the thought that to be unnamed is equivalent to nonexistence: "When the heavens above were yet unnamed, and no dwelling beneath was called by a name ... when no name had been recorded ... "

The parallel in Genesis finds Yahweh delegating to Adam the privilege of naming the created things as a symbol of human control (Genesis 2:19-20). The concept that knowledge of a name insured some measure of influence over destiny is thus deeply ingrained in these ancient cultures. The immediate corollary is that one's personal name must be carefully given and preferably have religious overtones. Also, such a name should not be unnecessarily disclosed, since the enemy who knows my name may share in the control of my fate.

Particularly among the Egyptians, the name was part of the person, in some ways equivalent to the concept of the soul. Many elect Egyptians had two names — a great or true name and a little or good name. Only the little name was made public — the great name was disclosed only to deity. A tomb inscription of a high Ptolemaic period makes this clear: "He was named Imhotep, but he was called Petubaste."

Although partly traceable to this Egyptian influence, the Hebrew
enveloped this duality with deeper religious significance. Abram had
been to Egypt before he became Abraham, but the Hebrew writer
ascribes the occasion to a special revelation of El Shaddai, the Almighty
God (Genesis 17:1-5). Later, Jacob becomes Israel after wrestling with
a messenger direct from Yahweh (Genesis 32:24-30).

In almost every ancient Near Eastern civilization, the search for divine
favor through a "proper" name was progressively reduced to a formula.
Particularly among the elite, each name becomes a grammatical
sentence, either fully expressed or implied, containing two or three
elements.[10] Almost a century ago, George and Henry Rawlinson
analyzed the names listed in the Assyrian cuneiform inscriptions then
available. In nearly a thousand names, the formula is confirmed with
but slight exception. There is a noun in the nominative case, followed
by a verb, and then a noun in the objective case. In addition, over two-
thirds of the combinations have the name of a god as the initial noun.
Of 39 kings, only three have names of secular character. Modern
scholarship would increase the proportion of names invoking divine
favor.

But what of Hebrew names? A study of a list of Biblical names,
particularly after the advent of the monarchy, will show a similar
disposition to include forms of Yah, El, Adonai, and even Baal and
Am. To make the application to the case of Jonah, we can detail the
names given to those designated as prophets *(nabiy)*. Of 61 named
prophets, in 38 of them the reference to Deity is direct and in 26
implied. Those names remaining — Aaron, Moses, and Habakkuk —
are of non-Hebrew derivation. The meanings of Jeduthun and Jerimoth
are uncertain, although they are both compound names. Only Iddo[11]
and Jonah are left.

Running counter to the names of divine incantation with Assyrian or
Egyptian overtones was the choice of a name from the natural
surroundings — particularly from those objects that had special
meaning for the tribe or family. About 1890, Dr. Robertson Smith

---

[10] Isaiah expanded the name of one son to *four* elements for dramatic effect
(See Isaiah 8:3).
[11] *Iddo* is variously thought to mean *timely, loving,* or *adorned.*

traced these influences of totemism in Hebrew culture. Undeniably, 33 Biblical names are derived from animals.

Based on the legacy of a dying Jacob (Genesis 49:1-28), Judah is a lion's whelp; Issachar, a strong ass; Dan, a serpent; Naphtali, a hind; Benjamin, a wolf. Those with totem names would be particularly blessed. However, animist names are principally from pre-monarchial Israel. There may have been residual totemism in frontier Galilean villages since they were exposed to a similar (and stronger) Syrian tendency.[12] It is not necessary to ascribe Jonah's name solely to totemism to admit that for a Hebrew to retain such simplicity would align him with conservative and traditional elements.

Archaeological evidence gives further confirmation from the time of Jeroboam II, the king most closely linked to Jonah. Diggings at Samaria have uncovered potsherds (termed *ostraca* by archaeologists) which are thought to be receipts for corn, wine, and oil consigned to the king's treasury. The names of both farmers and palace officials appear, and most are theophoric compounds. There is complete absence of direct totem names.

Another Biblical use of the word *yownah* occurs in the title of Psalm 56. Its meaning is so idiomatic that the phrase appears without translation in the King James Version — *Yownah 'elam rechoqiym*. Depending on the rendering of the second word, the meaning is "The Cry of the Dove in the Distant Terebinth (Turpentine) Tree" or "The Silent Dove Among Strangers." Its use in the title of the Psalm is probably to define the melody or meter of the song. Perhaps David's thoughts were on his boyhood when he memorialized his fear of capture by the Philistines. Some think the melody he used was a Hebrew lullaby. Did Jonah's mother croon the song to her baby? Perhaps on such a fancy was the future prophet named, departing from the usual practice of assigning serious names. When Jonah's parents named him on the eighth day after his birth, did they have in mind a bird or a song, or did they give him an unknown name that was changed to Jonah later because of his experiences? We cannot be certain. There is some further Assyrian

---

[12] The Talmud (Kiddushin) contrasts the House of Yownah with the House of Urbathi (ravenlike) during the Babylonian captivity. This is more probably a dispute between Hebrew and Arab elements than a contest of totem families.

evidence to be heard, but that will have to wait until Chapter 11. We
will find that it is quite plausible that the name Jonah is a variation on
the name of the Assyrian demigod Oannes, which means "recovered
from the water."

There is more to be explored in the full name of the prophet: Yownah
ben Amittai. Is the provincialism of the son's name a heritage from the
father, Amittai? Here again the translation should be simple, but it is
not. The link to 'emeth (truth) seems direct. Although there is nothing in
the Bible to justify the early tradition, both St. Jerome and Pseudo-
Epiphanius mention a supposed connection between Elijah and Jonah
based on the words of the widow of Zarephath that "… the word of
the Lord in thy mouth is truth" (I Kings 17:24). The earliest traditions
identify Jonah with the widow's son raised from the dead. Later some
held the view that Elijah's scholar-prophets became known as the Sons
of Truth and that Jonah was a member of this band. As such, his actual
father's name is unknown to us.

The simplicity of the name Amittai brings the same problems already
cited for the name Jonah. The problem is greater if we admit that in
eighth-century Israel the prophetic function was institutionalized and
could be passed from father to son.[13] Such a choice of names over two
generations shows an ingrained tradition not easily overcome by the
fashion of the day.

There are those who would consider the name of Jonah ben Amittai as
too simple to be real and would dismiss it as either symbolic or
fabulous. This is consistent with the overall view of Jonah's allegory.
The prophet is identified with Israel and the great fish as Assyria, which
for a time swallows God's people into exile. We must maintain that a
historical Jonah preceded any allegorical use of his story and that this
kind of symbolism does not enter into the choice of his name.

We conclude that if Jonah's name be Hebrew, it marks him as the heir
of a conservative, provincial tradition. In a culture where a change in
name was easily justified, he remained simply, The Dove.

_____

[13] Amos finds it necessary to emphasize " … I was no prophet, neither was I a
prophet's son … " (Amos 7:14). See Chapter 3 for the development of
prophetic cults.

2 Can Any Good Thing Come from a Winepress?

Development of Jonah's Character

My Brethren! Let us not despise
The voice of Jonah the Hebrew.
It does not become us, foolishly,
To look down upon his preaching.
It may be thought to be audacity —
It may be considered as madness —
But if one should call him mad,
He is yet a treasure of great wisdom.
In him there is perception and intellect,
Intelligence springs up in him as a fountain.
His appearance is contemptible and unadorned,
But his speech is powerful and weighty.
  - Part IV, 1-4, 11-16

The hill folk of Galilee had a saying, "Climb Mount Tabor and watch what goes on in the world." The adage reveals the dichotomy in the mind of the Hebrew farmer. He had come to terms with the growing industry and trade that had begun to erode his traditional provincialism by becoming at most a skeptical spectator. Such must have been Jonah's heritage. (For reference in the following discussion, see the maps in the Appendix.)

The advice of the elders fit in well with natural boyish curiosity — and Jonah must have come to know this mountain well, this "balcony of Galilee." The ascent was not easy. The limestone scarps rise steeply from the plain of Jezreel to a summit of "marvelous roundness" (St. Jerome) some 1,300 feet above the valley. Jonah thrilled to stand on the same height where Barak, hero of the hill country, had mustered Israel's might five centuries before. That day, when 10,000 stalwart men of Zebulun and Naphtali had routed the Canaanite chariots of Sisera, was the birthday of Hebrew tribal control in the north (Judges 4:10-17).

Facing toward the sunrise, Jonah would have looked across the purple waters of the Sea of Chinnereth[14] (later Galilee) to the cities of Trans-Jordanic Bashan, towered and turreted in their ravines. The volcanic plateau was reserved for the fertile fields of grain and for grazing lands of the celebrated cattle of Bashan. Here the men of Manasseh fattened the herds that yielded table delicacies for King Joash in Samaria and the fortunate gentry throughout Israel. Those who tended the herds lived on the curded milk and not the meat.

But Jonah could not long look eastward — the triple white tops of Mt. Hermon draw the eye irresistibly northward. There the glittering snow never completely melts. The waters that trickle from the furrowed crest are the real source of the Jordan river and, hidden from Tabor, the freshets that flow north to form the Orontes. There lay the "entering of Hamath" where one day (if the elders were to be believed) the yoke of Damascus would be broken and the frontier restored as in the days of Solomon.

On the western slopes of Hermon, the tribe Asher held uncertain control. The towns of anti-Lebanon and the narrow seacoast could never be truly Hebrew in outlook (Judges 5:17). Phoenician Tyre was too close to ignore, and it was the chief source of commerce along the coastal highway through Acco. Now Syria controlled the inland route. Adad-Nirari, Assyria's boy king, had lost the influence of his Babylonian mother and was looking greedily westward. Israel's trade was increasingly with seafaring Tyre.

Where the mountains meet the sea, the black hulks of the Phoenician ships hugged the Carmel headland. Southbound they were toward Joppa and on to Egypt under crimson sail — or again homeward, usually with oaken oars flashing, since the northing breezes were less reliable.

Tabor tops the Carmel ridge in altitude, though not discernibly from a distance. Behind Carmel's jumbled rampart lay Samaria, the "new" capital, now almost a century old. The escarpment is roughly quartered by three gray limestone passes. Jokneam and Taanach were strategically important, but the central pass guarded by Megiddo was the keystone

---

[14] The name is thought to be derived from the lake's harp shape.

for defense of both the plain of Sharon to the south and the plain of Jezreel. In tribute to that importance, the king's main chariot force was headquartered there, with 400 or more horses. To the farmers of Zebulun, Megiddo was The City. It was probably head of the tax district and center of registration for the hated labor *corvée*.[15] There the landed gentry, the captains of trade, and the increasing number of military princes built their palaces and insulated themselves from the pleas of the peasants. But Megiddo was also the haven when bands of Syrian mercenaries raided the farmland. Even then there were those unwilling to admit their dependence on the city who simply melted into the rough highland country until the soldiers departed or were driven away.

The white, dusty road to enemy Damascus led out generally north from Megiddo, skirting the western slopes of Tabor. The plain of Jezreel and its extension, the valley of the brook Kishon, is bisected by the ancient roadbed. The brook rises in springs near Chisloth-Tabor and alternately floods and dries to a wadi. The drainage is intermittent, and in Jonah's day the most distinctive feature of the lowland was the marshes that harbored the "fly of Egypt," the mosquito. Dengue fever and malaria were endemic.[16]

So, his eye tracing out the road, Jonah's gaze came finally homeward — to Gath-Hepher. There to the west, the hills of Galilee[17] form the crenated rim of a saucered highland. Today, the white limed walls of the houses of Nazareth occupy the central hollow. But in Old Testament writings there is no mention of Nazareth or of any settlement which can be assigned to its site. There is reference to the rim villages — starting with Gath-Hepher on the north. Daberath, Chisloth-Tabor, Japhia, and Shimron complete the ring. The hill country lay largely in the portion of the Promised Land assigned to Zebulun, although Mt. Tabor is the meeting place with two other tribal

---

[15] unpaid work forced on the lower classes
[16] In modern times the marshes have been drained, and some of the most productive kibbutzim of the new Israel lie in the valley.
[17] Galilee means *the circle*. The area Solomon offered to Hiram of Tyre (I Kings 9:11-13) was probably farther west in Asher. Hiram contemptuously called the towns *Cabul* (worthless).

territories, Issachar on the south and Naphtali on the north (Joshua 19:10-23; 32-39).

The hills of Galilee, cut off by the marshes and the Sea of Chinnereth, had an undistinguished part in the history of Israel. Only a few generations after Jonah, the prophet Isaiah was to refer to the hill people as those "that walked in darkness" (Isaiah 9:2). This relative isolation contributed to a back-country mentality that persisted to New Testament days. In those times, Nathanael, not yet a disciple of Jesus, asked with sarcasm (since he, too, was a Galilean), "Can any good thing come out of Nazareth?"(John 1:46).[18] We may ask the same question concerning Gath-Hepher.

Although there is no statement that he was born there, Jonah spent enough time in Gath-Hepher to become identified with it. A reconstruction of the place and time may help us to understand the young Jonah.

Again we turn to etymology for clues. The first half of the place name, Gath, sometimes corrupted to Gittah, means *winepress*. The country was dotted with vineyards. Hepher means *dug,* and the combined form can be rendered *dug-out winepress.*

Unfortunately there have been virtually no archaeological excavations to confirm that Gath-Hepher was indeed the central winepress of the area.[19] However, if we can judge from the findings of Dr. James B. Pritchard at Gibeon, construction of such a winepress was a major industrial undertaking, involving hewing out and removing over 600 tons of rock — dug out indeed!

At Gibeon, two separate grape processing areas have been uncovered. The larger has a wine cellar spread out over one-fifth acre of table rock. Sixty-three caverns averaging seven feet deep are cut into the rock. The excavations are deep enough for two layers of pottery jars.

---

[18] Tradition has it that Nathanael retraced Jonah's steps in Asia Minor and Assyria and finally became a martyr in India.
[19] Tel Get Hefer is near modern Mash-had. There has been no attention to this mound since minor digging by German scholars before 1900. Americans have a dig at nearby Sepphoris.

The entire area could store 25,000 gallons of wine, considerable even by modern standards.

Grape processing started at a level piece of rock where the gatherers unloaded the baskets. Nearby the maidens trod barefoot in the circular winepress. The example at Gibeon is three feet in diameter and two feet deep. Leather thongs, hanging from an overhead frame, prevented the girls from falling as the rock became slippery. The rim of the press is a circular trough, and the juice overflowed to a plaster-lined cavern several feet away. When the main press filled, the skins, stems, and seeds were dipped out to an auxiliary basin and allowed to settle to recover more juice. After initial fermentation, the new wine was channeled through a rock trough successively to two underground tanks with an ingenious opening between them for decanting the juice free of sediment.

A wine center supported many a potter's wheel. The recovered jars contain 9.75 gallons, the Hebrew *bath* measure. They have pointed bottoms to compact the wine sediment (lees) and could stand only in pottery rings. The twin handles are inscribed with the owner's name and location, *e.g.,* "Gibeon, the vineyard of Amariah." Even individual writing characteristics can be detected.

The wine jars were filled using pottery funnels, and a layer of olive oil was added to seal away air. Each jar had a clay stopper individually crafted to fit, secured with leather thongs. The caverns today have an unvarying temperature of 65°F, even during the summer. Thus did the Hebrews age their wine under nearly ideal conditions.

To merit the name "dug-out winepress," Gath-Hepher may have been a special excavation problem. Perhaps at Tel Gat Hefer or some nearby mound, more evidence of Hebrew industry awaits the archaeologist's spade.

The three principal products of the Galilean hill country were olive oil, grain, and wine. The rhythm of these crops metered the life of the peasant:

> *His two months are (olive) harvest*
> *His two months are planting (grain)*

> *His two months are late planting*
> *His month is hoeing up of flax*
> *His month is harvest of barley*
> *His month is harvest and feasting*
> *His two months are vine tending*
> *His month is summer fruit.*[20]

The fields were fenced with loose rock, and each Hebrew farmer called a plot his own. On the steeper slopes, the vines prospered, especially when the farmer had the industry to arrange basins and culverts of rock to make the best use of uncertain rainfall.[21] Often olive trees grew in the same field, their metallic green foliage contrasting with the red earth. To produce oil, the trees require cultivation and if neglected will return to wild shrubs producing small, hard berries.

If indeed Gath-Hepher was the central winepress of Galilee, it offered more contact with the outside world than the clusters of farm hamlets. The pottery making required skilled artisans who maintained contact with those of their guild in other cities. Raw materials had to be imported and the wine prepared for shipment. This commerce required scribes, customs officials, and tax collectors. Such specialists composed the middle class of the day, the most stable element in a society even as in modern times. They were usually recruited from peasant families and could claim little inherited wealth. So Jonah's boyhood was spent in an environment midway between that of indolent Megiddo[22] and rustic Shimron.[23]

Intermarriage between Hebrew and Phoenician-Syrian was frequent on the frontier. This was particularly true in the royal and artisan classes. Diplomatic marriages at the court were frequent.[24] Hebrew architecture, technology, and art were not indigenous. Because of religious scruples, the skills were imported — through mixed marriages.

---

[20] This oft-quoted inscription is from a limestone plaque, "The Gezer Calendar," found by R. A. S. Macalister at Gezer and dates from the time of David. The routine is typical also of Galilean farming. Quoted in James Bennett Pritchard (tr.), *Ancient Near Eastern Texts* (Princeton: 1950).
[21] Today annual rainfall in the area averages 28-32 inches.
[22] Meaning *army headquarters*
[23] Meaning *frontier post*
[24] That of Ahab and Jezebel was the most notorious (I Kings 7:13).

Hiram, the brass-worker, was of Naphtali-Tyre (I Kings 7:13). The Hebrew alphabet is Ugaritic via Phoenicia, and Asher's sons gained fame as scribes. Kenite proselytes operated the brass foundries. Although all the tribes were guilty of racial impurity (Judges 1:27-33), at least on the frontier, intermarriage had the virtue of increasing the available skills. The remnants of Canaanite culture throughout the land were of undistinguished heritage.

Jonah's tribal background is not precisely known. Early Talmudic tradition is that Amittai was from Zebulun and his wife from Asher.

But there was another influence pervading the area. In a rough terrain, the highest hills have special significance. Galilee is triangulated by Mt. Hermon, the Carmel ridge, and the twin hills of Tabor-Moreh overlooking the valley of Jezreel. Each of these "high places" had a history of charisma. Hermon was worshipped by the Phoenicians, Syrians, and their Hittite predecessors. As such, it was taboo for the Israelites to hold it in awe (although the Hebrew word *hermon* means *sacred*). Yet its presence on the northern horizon inspired Hebrew poetic longings (Psalms 89:12; 133:3). It promised that much-anticipated return to the Golden Age, when Yahweh would expand Israel's boundaries and the peace of Solomon would prevail.

Mt. Carmel was one of the centers of the Elijah-Elisha chronicle. There the prophets of Baal were bested by Yahweh (I Kings 18). This holy association remained through Jonah's day as attested by Biblical (Amos 1:2) and secular (Pythagoras c. 500 BCE) sources.

The hill of Moreh is best known as the abode of the witch of Endor, a necromancer consulted by Saul just before his mortal battle at Gilboa (I Samuel 28:7ff). Since Moreh means *teacher*, it may have been the site of a prophetic school.

Gideon's rallying of his troops on Tabor probably had religious as well as military advantages. To swear "by Tabor" (Jeremiah 46:18) was to invoke the certainty of Yahweh's ultimate triumph. But that byword was a snare for the unwary in Jonah's time.[25]

---

[25] Hosea 5:1 is an indictment against false prophets at Tabor.

The religious climate during Jonah's boyhood was tepid and permissive. Without exception, the religious history of each high place is a mixture of practices pleasant to Yahweh and those He abhors.

But the yearning of the people to venerate local shrines, never fully obliterated, grew again when Jerusalem became the symbol of a rival state. During Israel's waning days, the kings encouraged the people to ignore the City of David in their worship. The high holy places grew in importance.

In summary, Jonah's culture was a frontier settlement with visible military presence, agricultural-industrial in its production of wine and olive oil, communicating with caravans and seaports in its commercial outreach, and multicultural in its mixture of racial and religious traditions. Its son Jonah proved to be curious, resourceful, devout, resilient — and political.

3   Where Does Jonah Stand Among the Prophets?

Development of a Prophetic Political Faction

> I flattered him [Jonah] but he was not enticed,
> I sought to terrify him, but he trembled not;
> He was a stranger to a sword,
> He was superior to a gift.
> Between flattery and fear
> We placed this Hebrew;
> But he escaped from both of them,
> For both of them he despised.
> The love of money was conquered by him,
> The fear of death was despised.
> Every word which he uttered,
> Cleft the stone by its sword.
>   - Part IV, 27, 28, 31, 32, 37-40, 43-46

The Bible designates Jonah as a prophet *(nabiy)* and a servant *('ebed)* of Yahweh. Old Testament writers use some form of *nabiy* over 500 times to characterize the prophetic function. As indicated in Chapter 1, there are 61 individuals named as prophets. To judge by Biblical reference, those called "Servants of Yahweh" were a more select group. A total of 12 Hebrews are so designated, seven prior to Jonah's time: Abraham, Moses, Elijah, Isaiah, Ahijah (a prophet in the time of Jeroboam I), and Jonah are the only men given the dual title of servant-prophet. Jonah is in good company.

The Hebrew *nabiy* was formerly held to derive from a radical signifying "to foam" (meaning, perhaps, cataleptic seizure) but more recently it has been related to a cognate family derived from the old Acadian *nabu*, "to call." The trend in interpretation is therefore away from the picture of a mantic with emotional excess toward one of a dedicated individual, set apart and called out from the common people.

Old Testament usage supports the newer view. The distinction is carefully made between prophets on the one hand and soothsayers, seers, diviners, and magicians *(chozeh* or *ra'ah)* on the other. Although prophets offered sacrifices on occasion, they were not priests in the traditional sense because they were not necessarily Levites and Sons of Aaron. Samuel alone was a prophet-priest. At least in early times, prophets were called "by Yahweh" direct from the proletariat and from the unofficial classes. Thus the prophetic function was not primarily hereditary but charismatic. The prophet Amos (c. 800) has no apology for stating that he was "neither a prophet or a prophet's son" (Amos 7:14). Nevertheless, hc would have to become a prophet to gain an audience for Yahweh's message.

Although Talmudic tradition calls Jonah a Nazarite, there is no direct evidence that the prophets uniformly subscribed to either of the ascetic sects, Nazarite or Rechabite. Nazarite men left their hair uncut and abstained from wine. Rechabite families owned no property and likewise drank no wine. Like sacrifice, the choice of fasting and asceticism for a prophet seems to have been an individual decision, with the intent of carrying out some direct command of Yahweh or of achieving a specific purpose.

The absence of a strict hereditary dynasty of uniform asceticism does not preclude a rather early institutionalizing of the prophetic function. Modern scholars take the expression "cultic prophet" almost for granted. It explains the preservation of the Sinai covenant tradition, which probably came down as oral history until the latter half of the eighth century.[26]

The prophet-priest Samuel is a key figure in this development. Murray Newman regards this story of Samuel as an attempt to explain the emergence of the cult as an institution.[27] In this view a mediator was required for an annual ceremony of covenant renewal. This role was originally acted by Moses and successively by Joshua, certain judges, and Levites — heroes of the Holy War for the Promised Land. With Samuel, the mediation passes from an ungodly priestly line to a righteous *nabiy*, with Samuel in a dual role as a righteous Son of Aaron.

---

[26] The term *cultic prophet* should not be considered derogatory. The most devoted religious leaders have been connected with institutions.

[27] See Murray Newman, "The Prophetic Call of Samuel" in B. W. Anderson and W. Harrelson, *Israel's Prophetic Heritage* (Norwich: 1962).

Concurrent with the establishment of the monarchy, Samuel took care to begin a school of prophets (I Samuel 19:20-21). It is clear from the experiences of Saul that the leader of the prophetic school would permit no interference with his primacy as the spokesman for Yahweh. A good case can be made for an annual covenant ceremony at Bethel during the entire prophetic period down to Hosea, with the cult representative as the mediator.

For a time under David, the functions of prophet, priest, and king become merged in the euphoria accompanying Israel's emergence as a true nation. But even in that period, the prophet Nathan continually reminded the king of his spiritual inadequacy (II Samuel 12:11). The cult continues to act closer to Yahweh's will than does the monarch.

There remains the necessity of linking Jonah to the prophetic cult. Some would admit no prophetic function outside the cult — even casting Amos as the messenger of an Edomite wisdom group. The direct Biblical evidence cited for the presence of an active prophetic cult is its emphasis on the ethical contrast between the prophet of Yahweh on the one hand and the priest or king on the other. In the case of Jonah, there is no ethical debate preserved, the link to King Jeroboam II being completely neutral in this respect.

To explain the relationship of the prophetic cult and the monarchy in the time of Jeroboam, we must trace the emergence of the cult as a political as well as ethical power. As we have seen, this dualism was a legacy of Samuel. The emphasis of Nathan and other unnamed prophets during the reign of David was provincial and political. The commerce of Solomon had wrought profound changes in the Hebrew nation. Solomon deliberately assailed ancestral power by dividing the country into 12 taxing districts that cut across tribal lines. The agricultural system, with the family group as the basic unit, began to be displaced by an industrial economy where individual and craft skills were rewarded. The schism between city and farm widened, hastened by discriminatory taxation of farm produce and forced labor *corvées*. A foreign policy emerged to implement the trade that encompassed northern Tyre as well as southern Sheba (in Arabia). Rehoboam, Solomon's son and successor, had an opportunity to reverse the trend, but he failed to do so (I Kings 12:1-17). The union of Judah and Israel, never strong, dissolved with the secession of the Ten Tribes under Jeroboam I, who had been under the protection of Egypt. Thus the bond to Egypt, evident in the treaty between Solomon and Shishak and sealed by Solomon's marriage to the pharaoh's daughter, became stronger.

The division of the nation had some cultic approval. The account in the *Books of the Kings* tells how the prophet Ahijah, in a secret meeting with Jeroboam before Solomon's death, condones rebellion. It took no special prophetic vision to divide Jeroboam's cloak into 12 pieces and to give the young usurper 10. The evidence of civil strife was already apparent.

Jeroboam had more independent ideas. At the first covenant ceremony after accession, the king intervened. At Bethel, he erected bull images, which some scholars feel were meant to bear the invisible Yahweh on their backs. He delayed the Feast of the Tabernacles one lunar month. An unnamed Man of God warned Jeroboam not to commit further sacrilege, but the king persisted. He was partly dissuaded only after the prophet worked signs and wonders, including the disfiguration and healing of the king's hand. Then Jeroboam tried bribery and treachery, employing a false prophet. The Man of God died in what was apparently the judgment of Yahweh for the breaking of a vow.

Time passed, but the king continued to harass the prophets and thus dishonor Yahweh. The prophet Ahijah, the one who had counseled rebellion, then delivered Yahweh's curse: "Therefore, behold, I will bring evil upon the house of Jeroboam [the royal family], and will cut off from Jeroboam him that pisseth against the wall [fighting men, especially mercenaries], and him that is shut up and left in Israel [probably members of the prophetic cult[28]], and will take away the remnant of the house of Jeroboam, as a man taketh away dung till it all be gone" (I Kings 14:10). The earthy simile shows the relationship between the cult and the king at this time.

The literal fulfillment of the curse was not long in coming. Judah had been invaded by the armies of Shishak, despite the treaty, and had

---

[28] The meaning of the idiom is controversial. It can also be translated, "him that is bound or free."

become Egypt's tributary. Evidently encouraged by the pharaoh, Rehoboam warred with Jeroboam continually. Either Shishak's ambition or Jeroboam's courting of Tyrian help caused Jeroboam's years of tutelage in Egypt to be forgotten. Abijah, Rehoboam's son, continued the attack when he became king. Of particular note, Judah captured the cult center at Bethel. (I Chronicles 13:20). The Biblical account is without much detail, but states that "the rest of the acts of Abijah end his ways, and his sayings are written in the story *(midrash)* of the prophet Iddo" (II Chronicles 13:22). Unfortunately the writings of Iddo are lost, but it is evident that Abijah had prophetic approval since he "waxed mighty." His son continued to permit the influence of the prophets to grow by removing the altars of foreign gods, destroying images and their sacred groves. Led by the prophet Azariah, Asa gathered the people of Judah (including representatives of the captured territory of Ephraim, Manasseh, and Simeon) and had a covenant renewal ceremony (II Chronicles 15:1-15). This is an indication of prophetic ascendancy over the priesthood.

The Egyptian view of this period is preserved in inscriptions on the great temple at Karnak. The role of Judean kings receives scant attention, but the list of the northern tributary towns, including Megiddo, shows the damage inflicted on Israel. These campaigns were part of the effort of the Bubastite dynasty to anchor itself as the successor to the Ramessids. The new pharaohs were Libyan merchants with their power base in the Nile delta. They thus were more interested in the coastal areas of the Great (Mediterranean) Sea than was the previous dynasty from Upper Egypt. The northern reach soon brought them into conflict with Phoenicia and eventually Assyria.

Meanwhile in Israel the prophetic party remained active. Probably with cult support, Baasha[29] "a nobody," murdered Nadab, Jeroboam's son, within two years of his accession. The provisions of the curse against the royal family were carried out with dispatch, and not one of Jeroboam's descendants was left alive to threaten the new dynasty. The account in the *Books of the Kings* of the reigns of Asa and Abijah is not nearly so complimentary as that in *Chronicles*. The northern prophets

---

[29] His name is probably a contraction of Baal-Shamash, foreign deities so abhorrent that the writer could not bear to spell it out.

could hardly countenance southern occupation of Bethel — even if Judah's prophets had the king's ear.

Scarcely had Baasha usurped the throne than he forgot his beginnings. The prophet Jehu was commissioned to remind the king that Yahweh "exalted him out of the dust" (I Kings 16:2). Since the king was unmoved, the mortal curse of Jeroboam was revived against him. Baasha was explicitly to bear the blame for the murder that led him to power. The litany of blood repeated in the short reigns of Elah, Zimri, and Tibni. Not until Omri was installed by the army did a new dynasty truly emerge. By this time Judah was in league with Ben-Hadad of Syria, and Israel was pressed from all sides.

Omri tried to duplicate the success of David in establishing a new capital city[30] — but Samaria was not to be a Jerusalem. Omri made a concession to the farmers by buying the land rather than confiscating it. Although Samaria was on a hill, there is no evidence that it previously had been held sacred, and the new king refused to build an altar or make a place for the prophets. His line, too, soon came under the Jeroboam curse (I Kings 16:22-26).

Although underemphasized in Hebrew history, the 12-year reign of Omri was important. He quickly recognized the conflict between Libyan and Tyrian merchants and aligned Israel with Phoenicia to offset Judah's dependence on Egypt. The treaty was sealed with the marriage of crown prince Ahab to Jezebel, daughter of Ithobaal of Sidon-Tyre.[31]

This treaty perhaps permitted Israel to share in the tolls for the coastal goods going to Phoenicia and thus had support of Samaria's merchants. With the backing of the army and the merchants, Omri evidently stabilized the situation enough to risk expanding his control to trade routes east of the Jordan river. His success is attested on the famous Moabite stave where Mesha of Moab complains of Israel's oppression east of the Salt (Dead) Sea. But, according to the inscription, Moab's

---

[30] The time for changing capitals was opportune. Zimri had committed suicide by shutting himself in the palace and setting it afire.

[31] Evidently the two Phoenician cities were under a single king for a time (Josephus, *Antiquities*, IX, 14:2). According to Menander of Ephesus, Ithobaal, the chief priest of Ishtar, ended the dynasty of Hiram's house by assassination.

god Chemosh prevailed, and the sons of Omri were eventually driven back.

The interest of Omri in Trans-Jordan was a direct threat to the prophetic school. It is no accident that Elijah comes forth from "the inhabitants of Gilead" (I Kings 17:1) to speak for Yahweh. Unwelcome in Samaria and driven from Bethel, Israel's prophetic cult could flourish only on the other side of the river.

The confederacy being shaped by Tyre and the growing interference with trade routes could not be ignored by Assyria. Under young Ashur-nasir-apal II who ascended the throne in the same year as Omri, the Assyrian army was overhauled and equipped as an expeditionary force. The traditional infantry-chariot corps was supplemented with cavalry and siege machines. He started building a new capital at Kalah to supplant the one at Asshur. Bloodying his new army by capturing Dikanni on the river Habur, he erected a pillar covered by human skin. The chieftains and royal family were impaled alive on stakes and dismembered. It is no wonder that fear spread ahead as he advanced west through Harran and Carchemish. Ithobaal hastened to provide tribute that stocked Ashur-nasir-apal's new zoo at Kalah — 15 lions, 50 cubs, a great and little dolphin (transported in huge pottery jars), wild bulls, elephants, francolins, pagate,[32] asses, gazelles, stags, and panthers. Evidently Assyria established necessary control over its western trade outlets and strengthened Ben-Hadad in Damascus. But Omri and the petty states to the south were not enough of a threat to require attention.

In Samaria, Omri started a school for diplomats and scribes to bring continuity to his foreign policy. This originally had only secondary religious implications, although it clearly challenged one of the dual prophetic functions. However, with Jezebel's guidance, the young trainees soon became devotees of Baal-Melqart. Ahab's accession set the stage for a direct confrontation between the prophetic party and the king. Ahab had the city dwellers and the professional army on his side. The prophets spoke for the conservative farmers as well as for Yahweh.

---

[32] Mentioned in Layard's Inscriptions, xliv, 17 but *pagate* is unexplained. See "On the Mammalia of the Assyrian Scriptures," *Transactions of the Society of Biblical Archeology* (London): Vol. 5, 382.

Now followed the familiar Elijah-Elisha cycle. The detail of the stories reveals their importance to the men who put them in writing — no doubt sons of the prophets themselves.[33] Elijah is presented as a savior of Yahweh's people like Moses. He looms so large that, in later tradition, the Messiah can only appear after Elijah is reincarnated. Although the stories have considerable ethical teaching, the political aspect must not be overlooked. Elijah's feeding by the ravens (Hebrew *oreb*) can be interpreted as consultation with the Arabian Moabites. His sojourn with the widow at Zarephath was probably while on a diplomatic mission to Sidon. His visits to Carmel, Gilgal, and Horeb may have been to strengthen the high places of the cult (I Kings 17). The pattern is that, although Ahab is repeatedly condemned for his ethical shortcomings, he was encouraged in his political aims, specifically the attack against Ben-Hadad. The prophetic party grew in influence and had visions of a Syrian league to resist a reawakened Assyria.

In the spring of the year (probably 858), Ben-Hadad brought out his Aramaean army to again raid Israel. The battle was joined at Aphek, east of the Sea of Chinnereth. The Syrians evidently attacked along the valleys, but Ahab commanded the heights, and 100,000 of Ben-Hadad's infantry were killed in a day.[34] Ahab's strategist was a Man of Yahweh. Ben-Hadad sued for peace, groveling in sackcloth and ashes. Ahab spared his life, contrary to the advice of the prophets.

Ahab's temporary victory over Damascus furthered the Syrian confederacy the prophets had been urging. The party had already picked Hazael, a member of Ben-Hadad's court, as king in Damascus, but waited for a more opportune moment to install him. Assyria could no longer ignore Ahab's successes, and Shalmaneser III with his new *turtanu* (field marshal) set out on a punitive expedition in 854.

The armies met at Karkar on the Orontes, according to Shalmaneser's epigraph:

---

[33] Although the *Books of the Kings* were probably not written until after the captivity, they drew on the writings of Nathan, Ahijah the Shilonite, Shemiah, Iddo the Seer, Iddo the Prophet, Isaiah, and Jehu.

[34] Probably an exaggeration.

> *I approached Karkara. I destroyed, tore down and burned Karkara, his royal residence. He brought along to help him 1,200 chariots, 1,200 cavalrymen, 20,000 foot soldiers of Adad-idri [Ben-Hadad] of Damascus; 10,000 foot soldiers of Irhuleni from Hamath; 2,000 chariots, 10,000 foot soldiers of Ahab the Israelite; 500 soldiers from Kue, 1,000 soldiers from Musri ...*[35]

There are no Assyrian boasts of complete victory, and the usual accounts of massacre are missing, so the battle probably was indecisive — therefore a victory for the confederacy. It goes unmentioned in Biblical texts, though Ahab was the strongman of the coalition.

Despite military triumphs, Ahab lost support of the prophetic party. The story of his connivance with his foreign queen to rob a poor farmer of his land would normally go unnoticed had it not reflected the schism between the king and the conservative group (I Kings 21:11-24). Ahab did reach a temporary truce with Elijah, long enough to obtain his help in aligning Judah under Jehoshaphat with the confederacy. When Ben-Hadad resisted an increase in tribute, the prophetic party split over Israel's continued military involvement. This split between traditionalists and those prophets who regarded themselves as royal diplomats continued down through Jonah's day. Ahab died in a skirmish with Ben-Hadad in Gilead near the cult center in 852.

Ahab's sickly son Ahaziah succeeded him but reigned only two years. The Bible implies that Elijah was instrumental in his death. The younger brother Joram became king about 850. The confederacy was under severe strain from Assyrian pressure. Moab succeeded in revolting from the vassalage that Omri had imposed. Hazael, the prophetic party's choice, finally gained power in Damascus about 844 by murdering Ben-Hadad during an Assyrian attack. Shalmaneser says:

> *I defeated Adad-idri [Ben-Hadad] of Damascus together with twelve princes, his allies ...Adad-idri forsook the land [perished]. Hazael, the son of a nobody,*[36] *seized the throne.*[37]

---

[35] Pritchard, *Op. cit.*: 256.

[36] This is an Assyrian pun. *Hazael* in Hebrew means *El has seen. Ha-sa-ilu* is Assyrian for *son of a nobody*. We shall have occasion to investigate other such plays on words.

The traditional prophets induced the commander of Israel's army, Jehu, to murder Joram, and the house of Omri passed from the scene. Jehu and Hazael were not long in seeking peace with Assyria. Their tribute included "silver, gold, a gold beaker, golden goblets, pitchers of gold, lead, staves for the hand of the king, javelins." Assyrian northern trade routes to the Great Sea were reopened, and Israel's income from tolls disappeared. "In those days Yahweh began to cut Israel short: and Hazael smote them in all the coasts of Israel" (II Kings 10:32). Jehu had the support of the conservative element in purging dissident prophets, but he soon went his own way and fell under the curse. Syrian armies roamed the countryside even as far south as Gath and Jerusalem. Jehoahaz succeeded his father Jehu and evidently joined in the attack against Judah. A dying Elisha promised support of the prophets in ridding Israel of the Syrian who had been placed in power with both Elijah's and Elisha's blessings.

Israel in 800 BCE was politically defenseless. The Syrian confederacy was in shambles, and the former partners continually warred among themselves. At home, there was no prophet of the stature of Elisha to reunite the prophetic factions, one group espousing traditional ethics and the other, political accommodation. These were the conditions when Joash came to power in Israel, Ben-Hadad III began his reign[38] in Damascus, and Adad-Nirari, the boy king of Assyria, celebrated his coming of age by a drive westward. About 800, Jonah was born[39] — destined to be prophet (and peacemaker) not only in his own land, but also in the wider scene of Israel's travail.

We have no way of knowing when Jonah left hill-country Gath-Hepher. Perhaps his family was uprooted by Ben-Hadad's marauders, now in league with the Moabites from across the Jordan. Jonah probably entered a school of the prophets early in his boyhood and there learned the skills of reading and writing that were denied the common villager. Jonah thus became part of the intellectual elite. He

---

[37] Ashur text (M K A no. 30:25) in Gottlieb, Emil and Heinrich Kraeling, *Aram and Israel: or The Aramaeans in Syria and Mesopotamia* (New York: 1918): 79.
[38] Hazael tried to give his dynasty some legitimacy by naming his son after the king he murdered.
[39] For the present, the reader will have to take the chronology on faith.

also became identified with the diplomatic group loyal to the king, despite his conservative background. We shall see in the next chapter that Jonah was almost certainly assigned to the cult center at Bethel. During the first half of the eighth century, the centers must have been hotbeds of political activity as Israel sought a policy of survival among conflicting pressures.

Joash began his reign a pro-Syrian since he characterized himself as a "cedar of Lebanon." Amaziah of Judah was as a thorn in his side. "The Thorn"[40] had built up Judah's army by forced conscription in the two southern tribes. In addition, he had hired 100,000 Israelite mercenaries, principally from the border tribe of Ephraim. His campaign south to the Red Sea was successful, and he was as brutal as an Assyrian in slaughtering captives. He quarreled with his mercenary army, whose loyalty he questioned, and probably denied the Israelites their share of the booty. The army looted in Judah and Ephraim and virtually set up a buffer state. Amaziah entreated Joash to help him quell the rebellion, but Joash scornfully told the Judean to abide at home and not meddle with foreign campaigns if he wanted to remain king.[41] Amaziah ignored the advice, and civil war broke out between Judah and Israel. Amaziah was quickly defeated at Beth-Shemesh, part of the wall of Jerusalem was destroyed as a warning, and the temple and royal treasury were looted. Hostages were taken back to Samaria, and Amaziah remained Israel's vassal until his assassination 15 years later in 782. Southern Ephraim around Bethel must have been an armed camp during this entire period. Jonah had a front-row seat.

Joash was having his troubles with his erstwhile Syrian allies. For a time, Samaria itself was besieged and the famine was severe. But when Ben-Hadad heard the rumor that an Egyptian army had been hired against him, he and his army fled in panic. Israel followed through, and in three pitched battles, the greatest at Aphek, all the Israelite cities

---

[40] The cedar was a symbol of permanence and strength as the thorn was of weakness and submission. The word for *thorn* has a common root with that for the nose-ring or lip-hook of Assyrian captives (Ezekiel 38:4).

[41] See Edwin R. Thiele, *The Mysterious Numbers of the Hebrew Kings* (New York: 1951) for a somewhat different version of events.

under Syrian control for a decade were retaken. Sometime during this period, control of Damascus passed from Ben-Hadad to Mari.[42]

Adad-Nirari had made his mother Sammuramat (called *Semiramis* by the Greeks) his consort. She is described as the most beautiful, the most cruel, the most powerful, and the meet lustful of Assyrian queens. Her open exercise of power was also most unusual — for Assyrians took pride in male dominance. Adad-Nirari had some military success southeast toward Babylon and Borsippa, his consort's homeland. He was less successful in defending the northern mountain passes against the raids of the Khaldians. A series of punitive expeditions made the frontiers secure enough so that Assyrian armies could again march west. They confronted Mari in Damascus and decisively defeated him. The tribute exacted was huge, as the king inscribed later on his palace at Kalah:

> *The fear of the brightness of Asshur [my] lord, smote him [Mari] to earth, he took my feet and surrendered. Two thousand three hundred talents of silver, 20 talents of gold, 3,000 talents of copper, 5,000 talents of iron, colored garments, linen, an ivory bed, an ivory couch with inlaid border, his possessions, his goods, in unmeasured number in Damascus, his royal city, I took in his palace.[43]*

The Assyrian king had also discovered a way to end the dynasties of Syria. The captured kings were killed and all the male heirs so mutilated that they could never become pretenders to the throne.

Adad-Nirari was less than 40 years old when he died in 782, possibly of plague which his army brought back from Syria. Shalmaneser IV succeeded his father, but real power was vested in Shamshi-ilu, the new *turtanu* and former governor of Asshur.

Joash of Israel was evidently one of the few monarchs of the era to die naturally. Jeroboam II, his son, began his reign in 785. In the same year, Uzziah, a boy of 16, was placed in power in Jerusalem. His father

---

[42] Since Mari simply means *lord*, some scholars think it is just another name for Ben-Hadad.

[43] Robert William Rogers (tr., ed.), *Cuneiform Parallels to the Old Testament* (New York: 1912): 306.

remained nominal king for three years until he was murdered by his own bodyguard.

Uzziah was the vassal of Jeroboam in the early years of his reign. Uzziah had the support of the traditional prophets, and Jeroboam had the allegiance of the political group. Assyrian power was on the wane as the new king Shalmaneser gave attention to his northern frontier. The stage was set for the final resurgence of Israelite political influence. Jonah was to be a leading actor in that revival.

4   Why Did Jonah Flee?

Vindictive Divinity

Jonah fled from God,
And the Ninevites from holiness.
Justice placed them in fetters,
Yea, both of them like criminals.
They offered repentance to her,
And both were delivered.
She preserved Jonah in the sea,
And the Ninevites in the midst of dry land,
That as he was drawn out of the sea
He should draw out the sinking city.
Thus Nineveh, that stagnant lake, was moved
By Jonah who sprang from the deep.
    - Proemium, 21-28, 33-36

Jonah would have likely remained unknown had he not been singled out for a special mission. The start of the adventure is deceptively simple: "The word of Yahweh came unto Jonah." There is no mention of a theophany[44] as in Isaiah's call. There was no voice in the night as awoke Samuel. What was the word of Yahweh, and how did it come to Jonah?

Dr. Sigmund Mowinckel has analyzed the call and message of the reforming prophets of Jonah's time. He concludes that their powers rested on a forthright proclamation of the *word* of Yahweh rather than on possession by or action of the *spirit* of Yahweh, as in earlier times. The word has mental content; it can become known. It arises out of need and has constant attributes — the word is not capricious, wholly arbitrary, or incalculable. These prophets were pragmatists in that the word could only be surely known by its results. Even as it is today, confirmation of the word of Yahweh was a problem of faith.

---

[44] divine visitation

28

In the last chapter, we looked at the Near East political climate early in the eighth century. Shalmaneser III was beginning to press westward again when he fell to the plague in Syria in 772. About this same time, Uzziah gained uncontested rule in Judah, and relations with Israel improved. Young Jeroboam II began to dream of expansion into Syria and Trans-Jordan. During the next several years, he strengthened his rule at home and tested his armies against Moab. Successful there, he looked north toward Damascus. Any move in that direction would surely challenge Assyria's dominance. The *turtanu* Shamshi-ilu, a holdover from Shalmaneser's reign, kept the new king Asshur-Dan and the army occupied in campaigns south toward Babylon. In 768, rebellion broke out, and the Assyrian army was garrisoned "in the country." News of the civil strife spread along the caravan routes and reached Samaria. Perhaps now was the time to increase Israel's northern border to the entering of Hamath, as it was in Solomon's Golden Age.

Sometime during this period, the prophetic party, as custodian of diplomatic policy, decided that Israel must know more about Assyrian intentions. How much did Shamshi-ilu and the army dominate young Asshur-Dan? Were the rumbles of rebellion true, and what were the chances of success? Could Jeroboam influence the rebel leader?

The determination of Yahweh's will in these matters must have required lengthy serious discussion. It also produced schism in the group, re-emphasizing the division between conservative stay-at-homes and those who championed a more practical foreign policy.

This difference of opinion is clearly set out in the *Book of Amos*. Although the location of his birthplace, Tekoa, is uncertain,[45] Amos started his ministry associated with the northern prophets. His conservative views became unpopular, and Amaziah, cult leader at Bethel, bade him to prophesy in Judah, where there was less interest in northern expansion. The group at Bethel would remain loyal to the king. Amos took care to quote Amaziah's words that Bethel "is the *king's* chapel and ... the *king's* court" and to heap scorn upon it.

---

[45] Tekoa may have been an unknown northern town. There was a Tekoa in Judah, but it lay in barren country west of the Salt (Dead) Sea. Brambles rather than figs and sycamores grew there.

Out of the convocation of the prophets and the weighing of alternatives came the decision to send a mission to Assyria. We have no hint as to whether this was to be an official delegation or espionage. Jonah was chosen, possibly as the leader of a group. It is likely that the choice was deliberate and a compromise — Jonah was uniquely a conservative pragmatist.

Now before the reader condemns this admitted series of conjectures as not being sufficiently supernatural, recall that the method just outlined closely parallels the means of determining God's will today. The accomplishment of God's intervention in human history depended just as surely on people of faith in Jonah's time as it does in ours.

But the message of Amos is that Jeroboam will fail and that Israel will become captive. What is to dash the hopes of Jeroboam and his prophets? The intervention of the Thunderer, the Creator, the Earthshaker, will come in a great and terrible "Day of Yahweh." Amos uses figurative and symbolic language, but his message loses impact unless he was alluding to actual, historical events that have aroused terror in his hearers.

There are three virtually simultaneous judgments encompassed in the Day of Yahweh. The first is withholding the spring (latter) rains for three months before harvest. The second woe is a "darkness at noon," and finally, the very foundation of the Earth would tremble in a quake directed at the prophets who disagree with Amos.

Note particularly that Amos exempts the king from the direct consequences of The Day. The fate of his household is to fall by the sword. In the surrounding nations, the king suffers with the people (Amos 1-3). But in Israel's case, the Day of Judgment is particularly directed against the cultic prophets who have been Jeroboam's advisers. They may have been well-intentioned in their preoccupation with political activity, but Amos speaks fearlessly that political expediency is no substitute for social consciousness.

There is little evidence in Amos that the prophets at Bethel worshipped gods other than Yahweh.[46] By standards of the day, these were "good"

---

[46] There may be allusions to star worship in Amos 5:8 and 26.

men serving their king. Amos reminds them that they have a higher calling.

The drought and pestilence are to come three months before the harvest. What little rain that falls is to be spotty — falling on one city, but not on the next. The dry season in Israel usually began in the third month, Sivan, and continued into the seventh month. The spring rains in the first month of Abib had to be sufficient to mature fruit and grain for the harvest. The harvest was celebrated on the sixth of Sivan in the Feast of Weeks (*Shaberoth* or Pentecost) seven weeks after the Passover meal (15th of Abib). Amos is saying that the land will be parched from year's end to *Shaberoth*, and the joy of the harvest festival will become mourning at the hand of Yahweh — the songs will be lamentations. Droughts are mentioned so frequently in ancient texts that it is impossible to fix the year from this set of circumstances. By our calendar the dry season would be in April, May, and June.

> *And it shall come to pass in that day, saith Yahweh, that I will cause the sun to go down at noon and I will darken the earth on a clear day (Amos 8:9-10).*

There is no more certain date in Old Testament prophecy than the one on which this total eclipse of the Sun took place — June 15, 763 BCE.[47] Assyrian texts confirm that the event was in the month Sivan.[48] It would have been on the last day of the month, just before the new Moon. Modern astronomical tables confirm the occurrence.[49] The path of totality passes close to both Samaria and Nineveh. (It will prove significant that both Jonah in Bethel and the Ninevites in Assyria experienced the same eclipse.)

Although the Hebrews were not as superstitious as their contemporaries, the sight of the Sun being blotted out as it rose towards its zenith brought awe to all. Those bold enough to look at the

---

[47] This is the Julian calendar date usually found in references. The Gregorian (current calendar) date would be June 23.

[48] See Chapter 10.

[49] Such tables accept the ancient date and use it to establish parameters to correct other eclipses for small changes in the Moon's movement.

Sun-god in his shame were blinded.[50] You can imagine the questions and accusations as the people wondered whose sin had brought on this tragedy. All of the sacrifices and ceremonies at Bethel had been unable to prevent it.

But the third and most severe blow — an earthquake — was still to fall. Talmudists say it came within three weeks, specifically on the 17th of Tammuz.[51]

> *And Yahweh will roar from Zion and utter his voice from Jerusalem; and the habitations of the shepherds shall mourn, and the top of Carmel shall wither (Joel 3:16).*

The quake was particularly destructive in the mountains and thus struck down many sanctuaries and high places. The conservative prophets had a ready explanation. Yahweh was punishing the false prophets in both north and south who supported the royal ambition of conquest. The sacred places at both Bethel and Jerusalem were damaged:

> *I [Amos] saw Yahweh standing upon the altar [at Bethel]: and he said, 'Smite the lintel of the door, that the posts may shake: and cut them in the head, all of them!' (Amos 9:1).* [52]

Biblical accounts do not mention damage to Jerusalem's temple but do ascribe King Uzziah's leprosy to the judgment of Yahweh. Josephus goes further, evidently quoting an ancient source, and says the earthquake was simultaneous with Uzziah's transgression.

> *In the meantime a great earthquake shook the ground, and a rent was made in the temple, and the bright rays of the sun shone through it, and fell upon the king's face, insomuch that the leprosy seized upon him immediately.[53] And before the city, at a place called Eroge [En-rogel at the entrance to the valley of Hinnom to the south] half the mountain broke*

---

[50] Even after much publicity of the danger, the total eclipse of July 20, 1963 produced at least fifteen serious cases of eye damage in Illinois alone.

[51] This time is consistent with Amos's use of a basket of summer fruit as a symbol of Yahweh's judgment (Amos 8).

[52] The vision is of Yahweh standing on the bull altar. *The Interpreter's Bible* says a better translation of "in the head" is "by an earthquake."

[53] Uzziah, too, may have been a victim of sun-blindness due to viewing the eclipse. Leprosy as well as blindness was a judgment of the celestial gods. The Bible says Uzziah's symptoms were "in his forehead."

off from the rest on the west and rolled four furlongs till it stood still at the
east mountain.[54]

In modern terms the earthquake's intensity was about 7.5 on the Richter scale. It was so severe that Zechariah recalled it 250 years later as the supreme example of Yahweh's judgment.

We can appreciate the magnitude of the shock by comparison with an account of Dr. Paul Ilton, a modern archaeologist. He experienced a powerful earthquake — but of lesser intensity — while traveling to Nablus, ancient Shechem. Ilton describes the quake as if two express trains collided beneath him under the earth. He was knocked over, and his driver was thrown four feet into the air. Animals cried out in distress, fissures opened in the ground, and great plumes of dust rose into the sky.[55] It is not too great a leap of fancy to project this experience back almost three millennia and state that Jonah had an experience even more traumatic. We have it on the authority of Amos, certainly not Jonah's friend, that Jonah was indeed among the prophets who fled from Bethel in dismay. Some hid in caves, some climbed to the tops of mountains to attempt escape, but Amos has Jonah in mind when he says:

> *Though they be hid from [Yahweh's] sight in the bottom of the sea, thence*
> *will I command the serpent and he shall bite them (Amos 9:3).*[56]

So Jonah fled from Bethel to Joppa, not out of disobedience or out of fear of the consequences of the mission to Assyria — but in panic[57] from the judgment loosed upon the Chosen People by a terrible, vengeful God of Nature. He must have run all the way.

---

[54] Whiston, *Op. cit.*: 200.

[55] See Paul I. Ilton, *The Bible Was My Treasure Map* (Winter Haven: 1958).

[56] Jonah's rescue from the sea certainly must have been unique in his generation. We have difficulty finding a parallel in all of history. Amos reveals his bias when he uses two forms of the same word to express Yahweh's judgment: "I will command the *biter* to *bite* them."

[57] The Bible is silent as to why Jonah fled from the presence of Yahweh; Josephus says it was "out of fear."

5   Where in the World Was Tarshish?

Introducing a Deceptive Jonah

If he [Jonah] fled, where could he find rest,
And whither should he retreat if he entered a ship?
[The Ninevites] troubled him more
Than those who took him up and threw him in the sea.
How could Jonah conceal
The blemishes of the children of his people?
He completed his guileful conduct at the sea,
By his pretexts on the dry land;
As he falsely persuaded
The mariners when he took flight,
So he used lying arguments,
And constructed his abundant wiles.
   - Part IX, 111-121, 124

> *And [Jonah] went down to Joppa; and he found a ship going to Tarshish: so he paid the fare thereof, and went down into it, to go with them unto Tarshish from the presence of Yahweh (Jonah 1:3).*

The distance from Bethel to Joppa is 38 miles, down the valley of the Aijalon. The route was a familiar one to any Hebrew. Through the valley, the donkey caravans ambled on their way to the seacoast and the Philistine cities.

From Bethel, the road went south to Gibeon where Joshua had commanded the Sun to stand still in his battle with the Canaanites. As we have already described, Gibeon was a wine center much like Jonah's home town. On down the valley, the rolling hills of Judah give way to the Shephelah, a sloping moorland broken by ridges of chalk and limestone. The low hills are round, bare, and almost featureless. These intermediate highlands, balconied by the Judean hills, and in turn overlooking the coastal plain, were an almost constant battleground for the Philistines and Hebrews. Uzziah's armies had just come this way and established control of the coastal road halfway to Egypt. Of equal military importance, the Hebrews now had control of the iron smelters

34

at Lod and Ono in the Valley of Craftsmen, and were not dependent on the Philistines for their armor and weapons.[58]

At the seacoast, the river Aijalon is the southern limit of the plain of Sharon. The plain is wild and lonely, but the bright poppies, anemones, and narcissi (the roses of Sharon) are a contrast to the drab Shephelah. The road was almost pure chalk and in rainy weather became almost impassable, but Jonah had no worry of that kind as he hurried along. The long drought had made layers of dust that eddied in white plumes with every step.

Just before the rivulet reaches the sea, it meets the larger Kanah that marked the tribal border between Ephraim and Manasseh. Where the Kanah meets the sea is the site, now Tel Kasileh, of the unloading point for Hiram's cedar logs as they were on their way to become a part of Solomon's temple. The rafts were unleashed in the flatland to avoid Joppa's hill. The road Jonah traveled left the shallow valley and headed directly west toward the city.

Joppa is one of the few ports along the east coast of the Great Sea. The currents past the Nile delta bring the alluvium of Ethiopia to deposit in any protected harbor. This was not of much concern to the ancients because of the absence of tides and the shallow draft of their boats. Jewish legend says that the currents of the sea bring all the sunken treasures of the Mediterranean finally to rest in Joppa harbor. In King Solomon's time, the sea gave up its rich bounty, but it has been accumulating since waiting for the Messiah to distribute "to each man according to his merits."

The Phoenicians called the port Jaffa, the beautiful. In Hebrew lore, the name was derived from Japhet, one of Noah's sons. It lay on a rocky hill about 130 feet high, steep toward the sea, but gently sloping landward. It is the only eminence from Egypt to Carmel, and its cape projects into the sea, visible for miles. From Jonah's vantage point as he entered the city from the east, the wide sandy beach bent inward,

---

[58] During periods of war with the Philistines, Israel relied on the Kenites among them for smelting and forging. Iron was in such short supply that plows became swords and pruning hooks spears, as needed (I Samuel 13:19-20).

forming a small bay. In front of the cape and bay was a semicircle of reefs, forming a natural anchorage. The city was surrounded by sand dunes, but behind the hill was very fertile soil watered by two springs. The springs were channeled to irrigate orchards of pomegranates, figs, and apples, as well as gardens of lentils, beans, and grain. Here too were undrained marshes (Basset-Yafa), which aided defense of the city.

When the Peoples of the Sea invaded the coastal areas about 1200 BCE, they brought with them the worship of Britomartis, half woman, half fish. She was merged into the fertility cult of Ashtoreth to become Atergatis, or Derketo. The Syrian influence added the male fish deity, Dagon, to the pantheon. The religion that evolved was one of sexual license. Even in Egypt, Joppa was known for the beauty of its temple prostitutes. The outlines of the temple and its pool of sacred fish can still be seen at Beit-Dejan a few hundred yards east of the main gate to the old city. Legend says the fish wore ornaments of gold and jewels, though they may have only been of exotic species.

Joppa lay astride the Way of the Philistines, the route from Egypt to Damascus via the valley of Jezreel. In Jonah's day it was strongly fortified with walls 10 feet thick and up to 36 feet high. Every 100 feet there was a heavy guard tower, and the only land access was via the east gate, closed with huge wooden doors covered with metal and rawhide against axe and fire. No doubt the ruler of the city was tributary to Uzziah, but as a merchant port Joppa had known many masters. In the second millennium it was wholly Egyptian, but the invasion of the Peoples of the Sea resulted in local Philistine control. Then as Phoenicia became the chief maritime nation, the city's influence predominated. David's victories over the Philistines made Joppa the port for the new capital at Jerusalem, further exploited under Solomon. Joppa, then, was a melting pot of all the Near East cultures, and its merchants developed an attitude of business as usual, whatever the politics of the moment.

Jonah's goal as he entered the city was the waterfront, and he pressed on westward through the narrow streets.[59] Joppa's quay did not rival Tyre or Sidon, but it was active nonetheless. The long voyages into the mysterious waters of the setting Sun began at one of the Phoenician ports, and the lesser harbors to the south were feeder ports, mostly for coastwise traffic. Joppa was the port of call for two classes of boats, principally. The smaller craft were round, leather-covered shells used for ferrying and for coastal traffic. They were little more than open rowboats, without sail.

The workhorse of the sea, and the boat which Jonah sought, was a larger, single-decked craft, built up of pine carvel construction with plank edges abutting. The inevitable voids were caulked with bitumen, and the entire vessel was coated with liquid asphalt to discourage wood-loving worms that were especially destructive in midsummer. These ships had a built-up bow and stern — bas reliefs show them decorated with Poseidon's horse head and a fish's tail. Both the elevated structures were enclosed. The forepart served for cargo storage, and aft were quarters for the master, helmsman, and passengers of note. Since the boat was less than 40 feet long, the quarters were crowded. Carvings show about 10 oars on a side. There was one fir mast with a square sail of linen or papyrus. Cordage of the same material was rather weak, and the crew only hoisted sail in moderate winds. When not used, the mast and sail were taken down and stowed in a cradle.

The rudder was a steering paddle, and this, together with the rigging of the sail, prevented any tacking. Wind was of much use only when directly abaft the beam. At other times the sailors bent to the broad oars, used against leather thongs instead of rowlocks. On these small vessels, the men were not galley slaves, but a free, though pirate, crew who shared in the tariffs and the plunder.

J. Forfait, a French engineer of the last century, calculated that such a vessel under oar could maintain 4.5 knots for the first hour, slowing to

---

[59] Joppa is not mentioned in the Amos catalog of those cities appointed to feel Yahweh's wrath. We have no account of the effect of the earthquake at Joppa, though its inhabitants at least felt the shocks.

less than half that in a sustained voyage of 12 to 20 hours. The crew's endurance was phenomenal.

The largest merchantmen, called "ships of Tarshish," were infrequent visitors at Joppa. They were simply too cumbersome to use on any except the longest voyages. These broad-beamed sailing ships were primarily carriers of semi-refined ore, though they trafficked in all the goods needed to sustain the western colonies.

The Bible says Jonah's destination was "Tarshish." Josephus equates this place with Tarsus in Cilicia — recent writers guess that it refers to Tartessus, the Phoenician colony beyond the Pillars of Melqart. There were several cities of similar name — all ore-refining centers. The Phoenician word means *smelter* from a root signifying "to flow" — as does hot metal. Unless we wish to symbolize Jonah's presumed rebellion by placing Tarshish in a direction opposite Nineveh, it is difficult to pinpoint his destination. If he were to travel to Cilicia, he would board a coastal vessel in Joppa. If he were to travel to the far west, he would board the same vessel, changing to the larger ship of Tarshish at the staging point where the expedition outfitted — probably Tyre or Sidon.

By 800 the swarthy Phoenicians had colonies the entire length of the Great Sea. Every whit as resourceful as her grandaunt Jezebel, Princess Elissa[60] fled Tyre about 814 to settle Carthage (New City). Gadir (Cadiz) in Spain and Utica in Tunisia were already centuries old, and Sicily, Corsica, Sardinia, and perhaps lower Italy came under Phoenician influence in the eighth century.

Tartessus outside the Pillars of Melqart became a trading center whose inhabitants were the most intellectually active people in Europe between 1100 and 500 BCE. Their riches lay in the abundant metals of the Iberian peninsula — silver, gold, copper, and tin. After processing in the smelters that gave the city its name, the metals found their way to northern Europe by trade with the ancestors of Frisians, Saxons, Vikings, Dutch, and French. Tartessus became the mainspring of Mediterranean trade as well. Ships leaving Phoenicia took an entire

---

[60] Elissa is immortalized as Dido in Homer's story of *Jason and the Argonauts* and in Virgil's *Aeneid*.

season to reach the fabulous city and similar time to return. Round trips lasting three years were not uncommon. The relative value of metals permitted a Tyrian ship to leave its home port with an anchor of lead or iron and to return with one of Tartessian silver. The legends grew of the rich and easy life in the land of the sunset.[61]

There may have been a few Hebrew merchants in Tartessus in Jonah's day. Several centuries later, they were of sufficient number to merit special dispensation in the Talmud and were permitted infrequent pilgrimages to Jerusalem once every three years.[62]

We can picture Jonah bargaining at the quay-side for passage: "He paid the fare thereof." Even had he wished it, he could not have worked out his fare. His muscles were not hardened to the rowing duty he would have to share. The Phoenician sailors were more interested in silver they could divide than in a soft-hand they didn't really need. Jewish tradition says that Jonah had to pay 4,000 gold denarii[63] — enough to purchase the ship.

The fact that Jonah could pay his fare seems unimportant to the chronicle, but it does emphasize that here we have no penurious prophet. Perhaps Jonah had access to the cultic treasury at Bethel. He may have used the stipend the prophetic council intended for the expenses of his diplomatic journey to Nineveh.

Jonah did not wait on deck for farewells. He was off to his quarters in the aft cabin. There, gathering his robe about him, he was soon asleep on the floor. He did not hear the grunts of the sailors as they stowed the last of the cargo aboard. He did not hear their joshing as they cast off from the quay. So too, their sighs were for themselves as they bent over the oars and worked the craft out of the harbor and started north toward Tyre. Jonah slept peacefully — he was safe at last from the Earthshaker.

---

[61] Some scholars hold that Homer had this land in mind when he named the most wicked division of Hades, Tartarus.

[62] See II Chronicles 9:21 and I Kings 10:22.

[63] There were no minted coins in Jonah's day. Payment was probably in weighed silver shekels. A denarius is a Roman coin from a later period. In modern terms, the equivalent amount of money would buy a luxury automobile.

6   How Providential Was the Storm?

Forgiving Divinity

So He, the Good and Gracious
Teaches us by His reproof,
By His rod He makes known to us His love;
By His stroke He opens His treasure to us.
And though His chastisement is severe,
His goodness far exceeds it;
For His chastisement is administered
As a gift to the children of men.
Be comforted, ye mourning children,
And desist a little from your tears;
Soon the earthquake will leave us,
And the fierce anger will pass from us.
    - Part II, 162,163,166,167,182-189

As the Phoenician ship traveled north toward its rendezvous with the ships of Tarshish, misfortune was in its wake. The writer of Jonah says, "Yahweh sent out a great wind into the sea, and there was a mighty tempest in the sea, so that the ship was like to be broken." What manner of storm was this? What was so unusual that every seaman began to beseech his patron god for favor? Why did even the doughty Phoenician shipmaster fear?

Notice that the Biblical account is strangely silent about the part of a ship that was the first concern of any sailor in a blow — the sail and its rigging. We have already described how the coastal vessels were equipped with a sail as well as oars.[64] Contrast this account with that of the voyage of St. Paul in Acts 27. There we are made aware of every change in wind direction and set of rigging. This argument from silence is not persuasive, but it is unusual.

---

[64] It may have been that prevailing winds precluded use of the sail and it was furled. Today, July winds would be normally northerly. The trip south from Phoenicia could have been under sail, but there was a long row home.

The Hebrew idiom used to describe the storm is also unusual. Literally, it says, "Yahweh hurled a great wind into the sea." It is as if the writer were trying to emphasize the extreme hazard *in* the water.

The Talmudists (and later, Muslim sages) readily explained why the sailors feared this particular storm. The tradition in their day was that only the ship carrying Jonah was affected by the storm. Other nearby ships proceeded normally.[65] This would certainly have been a wonder to inspire terror in the superstitious seafarers.

> *A rumbling sound is first heard, and this is quickly followed by shocks under which the ship trembles or is so suddenly arrested in its course, that it produces the impression of grounding upon a rock. A number of such shocks may be received in succession, after which the ship appears to slide over the shoal and continue its course as before. When the lead is dropped the ship is perhaps found to be over great depths of water, so that the possibility of grounding is excluded. The sea is very calm before and after the shocks ... Though the sea may have been without a ripple and as smooth as a surface of glass, a shock severe enough to startle the crew from deep sleep and bring them rushing to the deck has not ruffled the surface of the water. Water appears to bubble up beneath the ship, though the surface remains quiet.*[66]

This author was not commenting on the adventures of Jonah but writing a scientific account of the effect of a seaquake on a ship. Often called a *tidal wave*, but more properly a *tsunami*, it is a phenomenon that frequently follows a severe earthquake in coastal areas. We can be reasonably certain that Uzziah's quake was no exception. Since earthquakes originate at some depth, the elastic waves are transmitted through underlying rock to the sea bottom as well as to the land mass. The quake wave velocity is much less in water than in rock and is refracted upward to become almost vertical. Successive seismic waves result in a series of compressional water shocks.

---

[65] In a Roman sea story. Cicero reports that Diagorus saved himself from being cast overboard as the cause of a storm by pointing to other vessels in the same plight and asking, "Do these, too, carry Diagorus?"

[66] William Herbert Hobbs, *Earthquakes: An Introduction to Seismic Geology* (New York: 1907): 239.

In a severe displacement with its aftershocks, the convulsion of both land and sea could continue for several weeks after the main quake.

The tsunami accompanying a seaquake has all the characteristics of the miraculous storm. First, it is unexpected. Even though Jonah, and perhaps the sailors too, had experienced the first tremors of the earthquake, they would scarcely believe that the hand of Yahweh would have proceeded out to sea — they thought they could flee from the presence of the Earthshaker. The tidal wave is not readily visible. The shallow rollers cannot develop the reach in the Mediterranean Sea that they do open ocean, but the distance between swells can be 50 miles or more. Such disturbances become evident only where the wave reaches bottom or surface obstructions. Truly, the storm could come out of a clear blue sky.

A tsunami is highly selective in its destruction. Over a submerged sandbar, a shelving bottom, or in a narrow bay, the waves may pile up over 100 feet high. If a ship is sailing above such a configuration, it can be caught in furious eddy currents from which there seems no escape. On the horizon a ship in deeper waters can sail by with no distress.

Aboard Jonah's ship, the master could not understand why his passenger was not awakened by the shocks. Already the mariners were throwing cargo overboard to lighten the ship so it could clear the hidden shoals that Poseidon had thrown up in their path. But Jonah slept on in his quarters — exhausted by his headlong flight from the earthquake. The Hebrew chronicler says he was not *shakab* (resting), not *tardema* (drowsing), but *radam* (stupified) — literally "dead to the world." The only sounder sleep is *yashen,* the final sleep of death. The writer of *De Jona Oratio* (uncertainly Philo) says the prophet was snoring so loudly that he could be heard above the commotion.

When Jonah finally emerged on the open deck, he saw the indecision of the crew as to what steps could save the ship and their lives. This is implied in the Biblical account but is strongly emphasized in Hebrew tradition. Folklore has it that the sailors, reluctant to sacrifice Jonah, let the prophet over the side several times into the water up to his waist. Each time they did, the storm ceased, only to renew its fury when Jonah was brought back aboard. This is perfectly explained by the periodicity between crests of a tsunami, which can be 15 minutes or more apart.

The attempt of the shipmaster to reach land is also a clue. The coastal trip between Joppa and the Phoenician cities was with land on the starboard horizon. Phoenician sailors "rode the night horse" only if absolutely necessary and usually kept close to shore so they could put in to a friendly cove for rest and sleep.[67] With sail struck, the captain ordered the rowers to pull for shore. The initial movement of a tsunami is an ebb away from shore. The withdrawal of water is as though by an exceptionally low tide. The sea sometimes recedes several miles, leaving mud flats and exposed reefs. These beckoned invitingly to the weary oarsmen, but they could not overcome the outgoing flood. "The men rowed hard to bring it to the land; but they could not: for the sea wrought, and was tempestuous against them."

Besides the storm, the other providential aspect of the account is the reliance on divine determination of the transgressor who brought on the storm. This seems to be at the suggestion of the Phoenician sailors, though equally a Hebrew custom.[68] Today, casting lots suggests throwing dice. Although knucklebones of sheep were fashioned into dice in these times, that method was not often used to determine lot. A closer parallel can be found in drawing straws.

Columbus must have had this scene in mind when his ships were in a violent storm while returning from the West Indies in 1493. The Admiral suggested a lottery to determine which of the Christians (the Indians were excluded) would do special penance so God would calm the storm. There was a chick-pea for each man, one cut with a cross. Columbus drew first and immediately got the crossed pea. When the seas didn't subside, they held a second drawing. The lot fell to an ordinary seaman, but heaven didn't respond. The third time it was Columbus again — but the storm continued. Finally, thinking

---

[67] On the dangers of sailing close to shore, see George Rawlinson, *History of Phoenicia* (New York: 1889): Chapter 9.

[68] Aaron's choice of a scapegoat is by lot (Leviticus 16:8), as is the division of the Promised Land (Joshua 18:6-10) and assignment of priestly duties (I Chronicles 24:31; 25:8; 26:13,14). The closest parallel to Jonah's case is the discovery of Jonathan's sin by lot (I Samuel 14:42).

themselves doomed, the entire crew vowed "to go in procession in their shirts" to the first shrine of the Virgin they encountered. And after that the storm abated.

It is easy to see in this account from the *Nina's* log[69] that the Admiral used the mariners' superstition in a way to best calm their fears and keep them diverted. The chances of the lot falling unaided twice on Columbus would be very small indeed.

The lottery on a Phoenician ship probably consisted in drawing round pebbles — the ill-fated one was black.[70] At the start of each day, the shipmaster took from a jar of mixed black and white stones a pebble to serve as the day's tally for the length of the voyage. If the stone were black, special libations of oil or wine or sacrifices of animals were offered to overcome the ill omen. So the shipmaster had plenty of stones available for the lottery. The black stone fell to Jonah — the stranger.[71] Was it Yahweh who guided the shipmaster's hand? In any case Yahweh's purpose was served. The frightened prophet was cast into the sea "and the sea ceased from her raging."

The sailors have one other part to play in the drama. If, despite all the evidence, Jonah was really innocent, they must absolve themselves of his blood. "They offered a sacrifice unto Yahweh and made vows." This was no simple libation of wine or oil, but more probably the sacrifice of an animal, blood for blood.[72]

In the calm sea, the oarsmen pulled hard to bring the ship about with its prow pointed homeward, and the crew hoisted sail. While the rudderman held the bearing, the master slit the animal's throat and collected the blood in a bowl. The blood was poured overboard and its pattern in the water watched for ominous shapes. If the ceremony was performed correctly, Poseidon (or Yahweh) would bring a wind from the right quarter to send the ship skimming to its destination. There is

---

[69] See Bartholomew Las Casas, *The Log of Christopher Columbus* (1960).

[70] The Hebrew phrase *naphal goral* is best translated "to divide the pebbles."

[71] Some have commented that each individual was harboring a secret sin and was equally worthy of the lot, but those are other stories.

[72] The ancients had respect for life, and inanimate cargo would have been jettisoned first.

an echo of this ceremony in the animal shapes that ornament our weathervanes today.

It is tempting to regard this sacrifice as a gesture of repentance and a resolve to sin no more. But this goes beyond even Hebrew ethical standards of the time. The pragmatic Phoenicians were simply acknowledging that following the suggestions of Jonah the storm was abated. Jonah's God, then, was the one who had been acting in the affair and the one who required appeasement. The vows might have been no more than promises that when they again passed the Carmel headland they would remember the strange Hebrew and pour a libation overboard to his God.

Before we resume Jonah's story, what of the effect of the tsunami ashore? In enclosed straits or bays, the quake sets up harmonic motions called *seiches*. These are very destructive. The island cities of Tyre and Arvad and those settlements around the bay now called the Gulf of Iskendrun would have been particularly vulnerable. Seneca (c. 500 CE) notes that Tyre and 12 inland cities were inundated on one occasion.

The prophet Amos makes clear that Uzziah's earthquake had similar consequences:

> *Shall not the land tremble for this, and everyone mourn that dwelleth therein? And it shall rise up wholly as a flood; and it shall be cast out [or up] and drowned, as by the flood of Egypt [i.e., the Nile] (Amos 8:8 and 9:5).*

The imagery is of a tidal wave and not of the rain cycle as the prophet proclaims:

> *Seek him … that calleth for the waters of the sea, and poureth them out upon the face of the earth: Yahweh is his name (Amos 5:8b and 9:6).*

Damascus, Samaria, Jerusalem, Edom, and Moab felt the power of the
Earthshaker. The Philistine and Phoenician coastal cities felt the
tremors, but they also felt the lash of the sea.[73] So Yahweh was
preparing the nations for the message of the prophet.

---

[73] *The Mediterranean Pilot* (1963 ed.) warns that in the event of an earthquake,
tsunamis may be expected to affect coastal areas from the mouth of the Nile
north to the Gulf of Iskendrun. Particularly destructive tsunamis accompanied
a Turkish quake in 1939.

7 Was It Really a Whale?

Natural Miracle

A fish bore [Jonah] through the sea.
But a chariot on the dry land.
He was humbled beneath the earth,
When he journeyed in the midst of the deep;
The sea was cleft asunder when he descended,
But the land when he went up;
The fishes of the sea there recognized him,
But the children of men on earth.
There was a storm in the abysses of the waters,
But a great tumult in the city.
The terrible monsters of the sea
Trembled on account of him when he went up.
  - Part VIII, 67-69, 72, 74-79, 82-85

We now arrive at that part of the Jonah chronicle that makes it unique
— the account of the prophet's preservation in the belly of a great fish.
We quickly join with those who point out that the Hebrew text makes
no specific mention of a whale. The word used is *dag,* most likely
derived from a root meaning *to squirm* and so general a term that it is
also applied to the small fish caught by a freshwater angler. The
references to Jonah in the Gospels are equally inconclusive as to the
species of fish. There the Greek does bring to mind a more monstrous
creature (incorrectly translated as *whale*), since the word is derived from
the verb form *gaping* and is distinct from the word used to describe the
Galilean lad's "five loaves and two fishes."

It is clear the writer of Jonah wanted to picture the fish as a benign
creature. He could have used the Hebrew equivalents of Leviathan,
serpent, or sea-monster to evoke the terror of *Tehom,* the watery abyss
of Semitic cosmogony.

However, Josephus refers to the great fish as a whale, and the Coptic
translation of the Prophets, made about 700 CE, uses the word *anbar.*
We see this word today in *ambergris,* a product of the sperm whale. So

the popular supposition that Jonah was actually swallowed by a whale is quite ancient.

The Talmudists (c. 500 CE) preferred to think of the fish as a special creation of God: Yahweh made this particular fish on the fifth day of Genesis and miraculously reserved it against the day of Jonah.

Some writers saw the interior of the creature as commodious as a synagogue, complete with lamps. In other versions the fish can speak, is transparent, or comes equipped with a great pearl in its entrails that shows the happenings in *Tehom* as on a television screen. Today there is little belief that any actual creature swallowed Jonah, much less one with all the conveniences just described.

Before attempting to revive interest in the proposition that a historical fish preserved the prophet, let us survey the spectrum of interpretations made to "explain" this incident which the author of the *Book of Jonah* clearly presents as a miracle. Most Biblical scholars today would attempt to dissuade us from trying to find any historical facts in the account of Jonah's preservation. If the entire book is treated as an allegory and The Dove as a symbol of Israel, then the sea-monster is the Assyro-Babylonian power that "swallowed" Israel. Since the book is clearly post-exilic, the writer may have had this example in Jeremiah before him:

> *Nebuchadnezzar the king of Babylon hath devoured me ... he hath swallowed me up like a dragon [i.e., sea-monster], he hath filled his belly with my delicates, he hath cast me out (Jeremiah 51:34).*

While largely agreeing with the allegorical interpretation, some scholars see Jonah as the Hebrew version of a family of myths. They point out a number of hero-monster confrontations which do have similarities. *The Tale of a Shipwrecked Sailor* tells of an Egyptian crew that went to sea in a ship 150 cubits long and 40 cubits wide. They went south, presumably into the Indian Ocean, where a great storm caused the loss of the ship with but a single survivor. He was washed ashore on a desert island and "passed three days alone" before he discovered another inhabitant — a vast monster 60 cubits long. "Its beard was more than two cubits in length; its limbs were overlaid with gold and its eyebrows were of real lapis-lazuli." After three months the kindly monster loaded the sailor with gifts and assisted his return to Egypt. Sanderson traces this folk tale to the discovery of a stranded whale on some uninhabited island.[74] The measurements fit a large rorqual whale whose baleen (whalebone about the mouth) might be described as a "beard." The lapis lazuli eyebrows may derive from the ancient belief that these stones were the eyeballs of sea monsters. The golden limbs may be a reference to the pale yellow oil rendered from whale blubber — truly a treasure.

Greek mythology is replete with sea monsters. One version of Hercules' rescue of Hesione, princess of Troy, says that the hero actually descended into the belly of the monster. He spent three days[75] cutting and hacking the entrails to kill it. A fragment of the writings of Hallanicus says Hercules' hair was singed by the intense heat of the dragon's belly.

Joppa, Jonah's embarkation point, was the scene of Perseus' rescue of another beautiful woman, Andromeda. The Ethiopian princess had been chained to the rocks as a sacrifice to the sea monster. Pliny reported to his Roman readers (c. 50 CE) that the inhabitants of Joppa still showed the marks of the chain on the rocks as evidence of the truth of the story. More likely the marks were made by the iron chain then commonly used to seal off such harbors from intruding ships.

Herodotus (c. 450 BCE), the Greek father of history, tells of Arion of Methymna, a harp player without peer. Arion was a very rich man and chartered a Corinthian ship for a trip to Italy (Tarentum). While underway, the sailors threatened to throw him overboard so they could seize his treasures. Fearing the retribution of the gods for outright murder, they gave Arion the alternative of suicide, in which case they would bury him on dry land. The harpist elected the sea, but begged to play his instrument one last time. The sailors consented. The music was so charming it attracted the dolphins, and when Arion leaped overboard, the sailors never suspected that the largest dolphin would bear the musician on its back all the way to Greece. When the sailors arrived in port and celebrated their ill-gotten gains, Arion and the city officials confronted them and gave them their just reward. Devout

---

[74] See summary of Sanderson (1939) in A. M. Husson, *The Mammals of Suriname* (Leiden: 1978): 515.
[75] See Chapter 8 on the allusion to "three days."

Greek sailors set a shrine to Poseidon, patron of the sea, at Taenarum. Herodotus tells that the Corinthians and Lesbians particularly offered libations at the bronze statue of Arion seated on a dolphin.

There is a closer parallel to Jonah in the Buddhist account of Mittavindaka, an Indian sailor. After seven days, the ship on which Mittavindaka was voyaging was divinely becalmed and immovable. Seven successive lots singled him out as the sinner, and the hapless sailor was cast adrift on a raft of reeds (or in some versions, a wooden plank) by which he reached an island of salvation. The ship proceeded on once the sinner was removed.

The folklore of most every seafaring people necessarily contains common elements. The Crusaders brought back tales from the Syrian port of Alexandretta and embellished them to create the saga of St. George and the Dragon. None of the stories extant parallel the tale of Jonah in any but a few particulars. We conclude that our quest for a historical Jonah should not take us back to some common, non-Hebrew source.

If myths do not satisfy as an explanation of the Biblical account, let's try a mixture of myth and science. That was the route taken early in the last century when archaeology was in its infancy.[76] The Philistine worship of the fish god Dagon had been well documented. Early excavations at Askelon revealed a temple, a pool for sacred carp, and nearby a supposed wine shop. The wine shop in particular was decorated with a fish design which led the German diggers to christen it the "Fish Tavern." While reputable scholars made no connection to Jonah, several popular writers jumped to the conclusion that Jonah's three days and nights were but an apologue about a lost weekend at the Fish Tavern. Soon German collegians had a new drinking song. Written by the prolific composer Josef Viktor von Scheffel, the first verse relates:

> *At Askelon in the Black Whale Inn*
> *A man drank day by day*
> *Till stiff as any broomstick he*

---

[76] See I Samuel 5:4. The stump of Dagon's fishy parts was discovered at Asshur.

At the marble table lay.[77]

The rest of the saga tells how the prophet can't pay his bill because his money was spent in a Ninevite brothel. He ends up tossed head-over-heels out the tavern door. This entire approach appears ludicrous and is of course satirical, but it is an example of the school that believes that Jonah was delayed on a diplomatic assignment and invented the fish story to placate his superiors. Rabbi Abarbanel, not wishing to call Jonah a liar, imagined that Jonah simply dreamed he had been swallowed by a great fish.[78]

In a more naturalistic vein, expositors have supposed that Jonah was rescued by a ship whose totem was the fish. There are bas-reliefs of Phoenician vessels with a figurehead prow, but the figure is universally that of a horse.[79]

Some ships did have a stern like a fishtail, and there is evidence that Cretan ships flew pennants in the form of a fish or dolphin. Similarly, Jonah may have been cast adrift in a whale-skin lifeboat or riding an inflated skin made of whale entrails. There are many references in Hittite and Assyrian annals of the use of inflated skins to ferry an army across a river. Early Japanese woodcuts show floats made of whale intestines supporting the carcass of a dead whale which otherwise rapidly loses buoyancy. But there is no indication that this was a practice in the Great Sea.

If a tidal wave actually caused the sailors' distress, as we discussed in the last chapter, there is the possibility that a beached whale carcass washed out to sea with the receding wave.[80]

Such a partially decomposed hulk would have floated, and Jonah could have clung to it for safety. Others fancy that the prophet rode on the

---

[77] Thomas C. Zimmerman (tr.), *Olla Podrida* (Reading: 1908), Vol. 2, 319.

[78] Alfred Jeremias, *The Old Testament in the Light of the Ancient East* (New York: 1913): Vol. 2, 305.

[79] The horse figurehead was a tribute to Poseidon the Earthshaker, whose totem on land was a horse and at sea, a dolphin.

[80] Pliny reports that M. Scarus carried the bones of such a carcass back to Rome in 58 CE. This curiosity had a backbone 18 inches in diameter and had been displayed at Joppa.

back of a live fish like Arion and cite the fact that in certain instances, as when nursing young or when wounded, a whale does not dive.

Another theory is that Jonah's salvation depended on a *product* of a whale's belly — ambergris. The chemical ambergrin, highly prized for perfumery, is present in the squid eaten by whales. The refuse from digestion, ambergris, collects in the intestines and is excreted. The pieces will float in saltwater and can be up to a foot in diameter and 5-6 feet long.[81] Jonah could have used such a float as a raft.

Having considered most other explanations, we now want to look at the more orthodox view — that Jonah was actually swallowed by a fish. We turn for support to the most current adventure of man and fish. Over the years a number of "true" stories have been cited.

In 1758 a sailor fell overboard in the Mediterranean. A shark attacked and completely swallowed the man, but a timely round from the ship's cannon caused the fish to vomit out its prey, and the sailor was recovered with no serious injury. The dead fish was also recovered and preserved. It weighed 3,924 pounds and was 20 feet long with fins nine feet wide. Since the fish was exhibited throughout Europe as a carnival attraction, there is little doubt as to whether the story is authentic. It is a fact that white sharks weigh up to five tons, and horses have been found whole, though quite dead, in their stomachs.

An oft-recounted incident is said to have occurred in 1891 to a certain James Bartley of the English whaling ship *Star of the East*. In harpooning a sperm whale, the whaleboat upset, and Bartley disappeared. The whale was subsequently caught, and the crew spent the remainder of the day and part of the night in flensing[82] out the monster. The next day, when tackle was attached to lift the whale's stomach, someone noticed a slight movement of that organ's walls. The stomach was slit open and there was Bartley — alive but unconscious. He spent two weeks in bed as a gibbering lunatic but was entirely recovered by the end of the third week. Later he recounted being thrown in the water and being "encompassed by an inky blackness." He remembered sliding along a smooth passage that seemed to move along his body. Then he

---

[81] Such a piece recovered in 1953 weighed 926 pounds.
[82] slicing the skin and blubber from a captured whale

felt less constrained — he had room to discover that the walls of his prison were slimy and yielding. Slowly realizing what must have happened, he went through alternate periods of coma and conscious sickness. He finally came to his senses in bed in the ship captain's cabin.

Bartley is described as a shy person who shunned publicity. The captain and officers issued separate and detailed accounts supporting Bartley's story. The incident was later investigated by M. deParville, a French scientist of note. He published the story in 1914 with these words:

> *I believe the account given by the English captain and his crew is worthy of belief. There are many cases reported where whales, in the fury of their dying agony, have swallowed human beings, but this is the first modern case where the victim has come forth safe and sound. After this modern illustration, I end by believing that Jonah did come out from the whale alive as the Bible records.*[83]

The evidence was reinvestigated by Sir Francis Fox in 1924. He was a hard-headed engineer and concluded that the reports are true, adding that he had calculated that enough air could have been trapped in the partially full stomach of a dying whale to sustain Bartley and seal out gastric juices.

Dr. Egerton Davis refutes any claim that a man could live longer than a few minutes immersed in the corrosive stomach fluids of a whale. He, too, remembers from personal experience a whaling expedition in the 1890s. He was serving a ship's doctor and, after a series of events like those described in the Bartley incident, he was called upon to dissect a whale's stomach to release a dead sailor, swallowed the previous day:

> *A fearsome sight met our eyes. The young man had apparently been badly crushed in the region of his chest, which may have been enough to kill him outright ... The most striking findings were external, however; the whale's gastric mucosa had encased the man's body (particularly the exposed parts) like the foot of a huge snail. His face, hands, and one of his legs where a trouser leg had been pulled up or torn, were badly macerated and partly digested ... The appearance and odor were so bad that all save I were*

---

[83]Quoted in Sir Francis Fox, *Sixty-Three Years of Engineering, Scientific and Social Work* (London: 1924).

forced to turn away, and we were obliged to consign him to the briny deep.[84]

In the 1950s a giant grouper made an attempt to swallow a skin diver of the U.S. Naval Sonar School at Key West, Florida. A group of navy divers attacked and supposedly killed a 500-pound grouper with spear guns. However, when one of the men approached, the fish with a great gasp sucked him into its mouth, up to the man's waist. He hacked at the fish's gills with a knife and was vomited out unharmed. The report notes that the larger Indian Ocean grouper can accommodate a man standing up in its mouth. Whether the man could emerge alive is not stated.

Although these tales give little evidence that man's survival inside a large fish is anything but miraculous, they do illustrate that the anatomy of quite normal species is large enough to accommodate a body of that size. There is no need to postulate a special creature to accomplish the swallowing — but there is need to consider a special preservation. For the literalist this is the essence of miracle and presents no problem.

But before we take the means of preservation entirely on faith, let us see which of the larger species might offer the most natural accomplishment of such a miracle. The trail leads directly to the sperm whale.

Because of its gigantic bulk, the blue whale was first accepted by fundamentalist enquirers as Jonah's fish. Scientists stated flatly that Biblical authority was completely nonfactual. The wave of scientific criticism in the early 19th century demanded proof. Investigation showed that the gullet of the blue whale is larger than that of an adult human. As the sperm whale became more hunted, reports were frequent that its throat could indeed accommodate a man. But naturalists struck back that the sperm whale was unknown in the Mediterranean Sea.

Archaeology unwittingly gave an assist to the fundamentalists. A cuneiform inscription by the Assyrian Tiglath Pileser I (c. 1106 BCE) most certainly refers to a whale hunt:

---

[84] Richard L. Golden, (ed.), *The Works of Egerton Yorrick Davis, MD* (Montreal: 1999).

> Ninip and Nergal [Assyrian gods], who bravery love, and the beasts of
> the field have entrusted to him [the king], and in the ships of Arvad he
> rode; a blower in the great sea he slew. Wild bulls destructive and fine ...

The blower *(nakhiru)* has been shown by etymological researches to signify especially the sperm whale. This is confirmed by bas reliefs uncovered on the gates of the city of Asshur, showing two spouting whales, their square heads typically those of the sperm variety.

Phoenicians in Jonah's time hunted sperm whale principally for ivory. Their tribute to Ashur-nasir-pal II (884-860 BCE) was "teeth of the blowers, the produce of the sea." So sperm whales were relatively abundant in ancient times. It may have been that part of the ivory for Ahab's palaces came from the sea.[85]

The sperm whale has another characteristic essential to the unique role we are investigating. It is a breathing mammal. Large fish outside the whale family are dependent on gills. We are just beginning to appreciate the breathing organs of the sperm whale. It has long been known that the whale must surface to inhale through the hole in the top of its head — and the oily mist-spume as it exhales gives rise to the cry, "Thar she blows!"

These are but the external signs of a delicate and complicated pressure-balancing mechanism that permits the sperm whale to dive to 500 fathoms in minutes with no apparent discomfort similar to "the bends" suffered by human divers. This means there must be provision to prevent nitrogen entering the blood under tons of pressure. The key to this regulation appears to be the spermaceti oil stored in the whale's cavernous skull. When aerated to a stable foam as the whale inhales, the oil absorbs nitrogen and finally carbon dioxide much more rapidly than it does oxygen. Moreover, this absorption increases as the pressure mounts so that, the deeper the whale dives, the higher the oxygen content in its lungs. There is also evidence that sperm blood contains beneficial parasites including bacteria which feed on nitrogen and excrete oxygen, permitting longer dives before replenishment of air.

---

[85] I Kings 22:39. Specimens of this ivory have been recovered, but as yet no one has determined the source.

The skull, sinus cavities, and upper trachea of the sperm whale act in the same manner as a diving bell, maintaining an oxygen pressure commensurate with the depth of water above. Temperature measurements indicate this part of the whale's body stays about 90°F, regardless of the water temperature.

Further studies of whale anatomy would lend further details to and perhaps even amend this description, but we hazard that there is a good chance for human survival in such an oxygen-rich environment.

No violence is done the Scriptures by supposing that Jonah was trapped in the breathing passages of a sperm whale rather than in its belly. The Hebrew word for *belly* simply denotes the soft entrails and could mean any part of the creature's insides. Another miracle — involving congruence of time, place, and purpose — remains.

8   How Long Is Three Days and Three Nights?

Resurrection and Rebirth: Jonah's Character Changes

Jonah went down to the sea and troubled it;
He ascended to the dry land and terrified it:
By a watery pathway he went down,
But ascended by a dry one.
The sea raged when he fled away;
When he preached the dry land was agitated.
By prayer the sea was quieted,
The dry land also by repentance.
He offered a prayer in the great fish,
And the Ninevites in the mighty city.
Prayer set Jonah at liberty,
And supplication the Ninevites.
   - Proemium, 11-20; VIII, 80,81

> *... and Jonah was in the belly of the fish three days and three nights (Jonah 1:17b).*

If we accept Jonah's sojourn in the fish as literal, though miraculous, must we also accept the duration as a period of 72 hours? Some, thinking to make the miracle more understandable, say that the literal meaning could be satisfied by a certain period of 37 hours containing parts of three days or nights. But, as Rev. Thomas Scott remarked in 1856, such calculations "scarcely justify the redundancy of 'three days and three nights.'"

Interpretation is hardly clarified by the New Testament reference:

> *... as Jonah was three days and three nights in the whale's belly; so shall the Son of man be three days and three nights in the heart of the earth (Matthew 12:40).*

There have been too many theories accounting for a literal fulfillment of this prophecy in Christ's death and resurrection to study here. There

57

is difficulty in maintaining a Friday crucifixion and a resurrection early Sunday morning. There is no such problem in the Jonah account, since the specific days cannot be deduced.

The phrase "three days and three nights" occurs often enough in Near Eastern literature as to deserve special study. The most ancient theme connects the time period to the disappearance of the waning Moon. The dark Moon time of three nights, though recurring and predictable, was a period of foreboding and sorrow. The reappearance of the thin crescent was not only the beginning of a new month, and hence auspicious, but also a time of joy and feasting. The Hebrews were not exempt from this influence. Amos singles out for scorn (Amos 8:4-6) those merchants who would transgress the solemn days of new Moon. Hosea, another prophet contemporary with Jonah, proclaims that because of Israel's infidelity, Yahweh "will also cause all her mirth to cease, her feast days, her new moons, her Sabbaths, and all her solemn feasts" (Hosea 2:11). Isaiah says Yahweh hates "your new moons and your appointed feasts" (Isaiah 1:14).

Although the darkened Moon gave rise to the early superstitions involving any three-day disappearance, in the later times we are considering, the symbolism was so pervasive that its use need not be a reference to a lunar cult. Since the mythical context is invariably death and the netherworld, the later Semites translated this to mean that the souls or shades of each departed soul lingered near the body for three days and three nights. Hebrew burial preparation involved no embalming, but only washing, perfuming, and binding the body. Hebrew law required speedy burial, within 24 hours, so that the body was removed out of sight before decomposition started.[86] There must have been infrequent occasions when coma or catalepsy were mistaken for death and "resurrection" followed. Folklore fastened on three days as the time of irrevocable death — after that time the spirit was so far into the netherworld that the journey could not be retraced without divine help.

This theme is recurrent in the most culturally widespread ancient myth of the Near East — "The Descent of Inanna to the Netherworld."

---

[86] Genesis 23:3-4.

This goddess of fertility was also known as Astarte, Tanit, Ishtar, and Amphitrite. We recount the Sumerian version, but there are later counterparts in Assyrian, Babylonian, Hittite, and Greek literature.

Inanna, goddess of love and war and queen of heaven, decides to add the netherworld to her kingdom and to awake the dead. She adorns herself in her richest robes and jewels and leaves instructions with her patron, the demigod Nin-shubur, that if she has not returned after three days and three nights, she will require divine aid. In that case Nin-shubur is to enlist the help of the gods of air, Moon, and water (Enlil, Narma, and Enki) so that Inanna can defeat her older sister, Eresh-kigel, goddess of death and gloom. As Inanna passes through the seven gates of the netherworld, she is forced to leave a ransom et each. Naked, stripped of her clothes and jewels, she faces the demon judges within the seventh gate. When her plan of conquest is uncovered, the demons fasten on her the Eye of Death, and her corpse is impaled on a stake.

Back on Earth, only Enki the water god agrees to assist. He devises an intricate plan to revive and rescue Inanna — but the plan must be executed in exact detail. The resurrection of Inanna succeeds, but through a mischance, demons accompany her return. They have instructions to bring Inanna back if she does not provide a substitute soul to satisfy the Eye of Death. At every earthly city she visits, the terrified god of the city grovels in sackcloth and ashes to avoid being consigned to death. Inanna cannot bear to let the demons execute judgment in the face of such humility. So the goddess returns home to prepare herself for return to the dead. There she finds her consort Dumuzi (Tammuz) celebrating and rejoicing in her absence. Enraged, the love-goddess condemns her lover, and the demons carry him away. The later versions add the resurrection of Dumuzi by a repentant Inanna.

There are some echoes of this myth in the song of Jonah from the fish's belly — although the Hebrew psalm is on a higher ethical plane. The picture is of Jonah descending to Sheol — the abode of the dead in the center of the Earth "at the bottoms of the mountains." "The (seven) bars of Earth" were about him. The journey's lasting three days and three nights has put him beyond all human help. Salvation from corruption can and does come from Yahweh. Therefore, vows and sacrifices will have to be paid as ransom.

There are not many who ascribe the psalm of Jonah 2 directly to the prophet. Even Martin Luther opined that "Jonah hardly felt so well as to sing so fine a song." Dr. Paul Haupt ascribes it to later insertion as he does the song of Hannah (I Samuel 2:1-10) and the song of Moses (Exodus 15:1-19). Although there are allusions to at least seven psalms, the majority composed by the Sons of Korah, there are Aramaeisms that point to the Maccabean era as the time of composition. This late date need not cause concern. Regardless of its source, the psalm must have been consistent with the tone of the other documents and traditions available to the compiler. The psalm is present in the form we have it in the numerous copies of the Twelve Prophets, recovered from the caves of the Qumran community (c. 100 BCE - 100 CE).

The *Book of Hymns* from the Qumran (or Dead Sea) Scrolls shows further how the "Descent to Sheol" had pervaded Hebrew thought:

For lo, the wall shall rock
>*unto its prime foundation,*
>*even as rocks a ship*
>*storm-tossed on the waters.*

The heavens shall thunder loud,
>*and they that now do dwell*
>*on the crumbling dust of the earth*
>*be as sailors on the seas,*
>*aghast at the roaring of the waters;*

All the wise men thereof
>*shall be as mariners on the deep*
>*when all their skill is confounded*
>*by the roaring of the seas,*
>*the seething of the depths,*
>*the swirling of the tides.*

High shall the billows [surge],
>*loud the breakers roar;*
>*and even as they surge,*
>*the Gates of Sheol shall be opened,*

Perdition's shafts be loosed.

Down shall they go screaming to the Abyss,
and the Gates of Sheol shall open
upon all worthless things.

The doors of Perdition
shall close on all iniquity
which they would yet bring forth;

The bars of eternity on all unworthy intent.
- Book of Hymns III:13-18.

My soul was overwhelmed
like them that go down to Sheol,

My spirit was sunken low amid the dead.

My life had reached the Pit

My soul waxed faint day and night without rest.
- Book of Hymns VIII:29

I was a sailor in a ship
when the seas did froth and foam,

All the breakers thereof kept pounding against me
and the whirlwind blow about me,
[and there was no] moment of calm
wherein to catch my breath,

Neither could I steer a course upon the waters;

The deeps echoed by groaning,
and I [came near] to the Gates of Death.
- Book of Hymns VI:22-25

Those who wish to be most conservative in Scriptural interpretation say that Jonah was in the fish's belly, that he died physically, and that God's miracle included Jonah's resurrection. Such exposition makes Jonah's experience the literal antecedent for the resurrection of the Messiah. Our own conclusion is that the time factor was met in the Hebrew idiom as soon as Jonah went beyond human help — whether the time period was hours or days. Whatever the duration, Jonah knew beyond doubt that he had been party to a miracle.

> ... and Yahweh spake unto the fish and it vomited out Jonah upon the dry land (Jonah 2:10).

The prophet's first thought was probably, "Where am I?" We have fewer clues than Jonah did. Josephus tells us that the whale transport ended on the shores of the Euxine (Black) Sea. This would have required further miracle since those waters are so saturated with sulfide that only mollusks and small fish near the surface can survive. Lebanese sailors have no doubts about the matter. They point out the white "Pillars of Jonah" on the shore of the Gulf of Iskendrun. A spur of the Amanus river descends there, leaving only a narrow, rocky passage between the hills and the sea. At this point stands a ruined archway whose white pillars are ships' landmarks. Beyond the gate the plain widens, and there are two defense walls.

The arch is of black and white marble, probably built by Justinian in commemoration of his victory on the plain of Pinarus in 530 CE. In the days of the Crusades, the strategic location made it a seat of customs. How the gateway became linked to Jonah, other than by general location, is lost in antiquity. The tradition goes back at least several centuries.

Six miles north of Saida (Sidon) is *Younes* (Mount of Jonah) that Muslim tradition says is the spot where the fish discharged Jonah. Nearby is the site of a village that ancients called Porphyreon, reflecting its fame as a center of murex fishing. Murex are the snail-like mollusks from which the Phoenicians obtained purple dye. The discarded shells cover the slopes of *Nebi Younes*, although there has been little careful excavation. In antiquity, the seaport may have been a whaling village as well and thus have been incorporated into oral tradition surrounding the story of Jonah.

Most probably the voyage from Joppa to Tarshish ended for the prophet on a sandy beach in northern Phoenicia.

9 How Far Is a Three-Day Journey?

The Lands Between Israel and Assyria

For even heroes now are trembling
At the mighty rumor which is proclaimed abroad.
One Hebrew now conquers us
Who have conquered so many:
Nineveh, the mother of heroes,
Is afraid of a solitary feeble one.
The lioness in her lair
Trembles at the Hebrew.
Asshur has roared against the world,
But the voice of Jonah roars against her.
Behold the race of Nimrod — the mighty one —
Is altogether brought low!
  - Part III, 74-77, 82-89

> *And the word of Yahweh came unto Jonah the second time, saying, "Arise and go unto Nineveh, that great city, and preach unto it the preaching that I bid thee." And Jonah arose and went unto Nineveh, according to the word of Yahweh. Now Nineveh was an exceeding great city of three days' journey (Jonah 3:1-3).*

How long did Jonah lie on that Phoenician beach recovering from Yahweh's submarine ride? We have no clue. Tradition (especially Josephus) says he "was without any hurt upon his body," but the Koran states that "God cast him on a bare shore and he was sick." In either case, this was a time of introspection and reflection. Was Yahweh really angry with his prophets? Wherein had Jonah failed his king and his God? The destruction Jonah had witnessed on his flight to Joppa, the marks of the rampaging water on this desolate beach — surely the Earthshaker's message was to a broader audience than the prophet alone. In their fear the Hebrew people had been misled. Their agitation against the Servants of Yahweh had been a mistake — the proof was in the salvation of the chief sinner (so Jonah thought of himself) from Sheol.

All around was the jetsam of the receded tsunami. Here were chests and vessels far removed from their normal storerooms. There were wrecked slips on the sloping beaches where ships had been drawn out of the water for caulking and resealing with bitumen. The tar vats were overturned, and their contents now hung in blackened festoons to clothe the tamarisk trees and acacia bushes in mourning.

The tidal wave did produce one temporary improvement. The salty waters had washed away the garlic stench of the dye works. The loose murex shells, once piled twice the height of a man, were scattered about, though the mound that marked centuries of industry remained. The stone crushing floor where the flesh of the mollusk was smashed to release the purple gland was washed clean. The lead cauldrons used to produce lye from wood ashes and finally to render out the purple extract from the lye-gland mixture were undisturbed. But the complicated pottery piping that led from the brass kettles to furnish steam to the vat (the first boiler plants) lay in disarray. The skilled attendants, their bodies blue from exposure to the fumes that normally pervaded the atmosphere, had fled or were drowned in the quick onrush of the wave. It would he many moons before Tyrian purple would again be a staple for their merchants on sea and land.

The few inland cities (so obscure we don't know them by name) and the more sheltered coastal cities of Byblus and Sidon probably recovered first.[87] The exposed island kingdoms of Tyre and Arvad with their multi-storied "skyscrapers" would require almost complete rebuilding. The peninsular tail of Iatnana (Cyprus) had directed much of the wave's energy at the open mouth of the Gulf of Issus (Iskendrun), setting up a seiche with crests over 70 cubits high. We can be sure that any early counterparts of Jonah's Pillars did not stand against that onslaught.

The sages of Islam, drawing on ancient sources, say that Allah provided special sustenance for the truant prophet. In a manner reminiscent of Elijah and the ravens, Jonah was suckled by an antelope, a goat, or a gazelle. The various versions differ as to the animal. As in the Elijah

---

[87] Sidon was particularly well protected by a natural reef and causeway.

chronicle, [88] there is at least the hint that the benefactor was human rather than animal.

Some scholars surmise that Jonah began his missionary efforts directly on the coast of Phoenicia. The archaeologist H. Clay Trumbull, editor of *The Sunday School Times* and a missionary himself, said:

> *What better heralding, as a divinely sent messenger to Nineveh, could Jonah have had, than to be thrown up out of the mouth of a great fish, in the presence of witnesses, say, on the coast of Phoenicia, where the fish-god was a favorite object of worship? Such an incident would have inevitably aroused the mercurial nature of Oriental observers, so that a multitude would be ready to follow the seemingly new avatar of the fish-god, proclaiming his uprising from the sea.*[89]

If Jonah told the Phoenicians of his miraculous salvation, the Bible does not record it. In the face of such widespread destruction, practically every survivor had a story to tell, and the prophet would have had to vie for attention.

"And the word of Yahweh came the second time" implies a discontinuity. We can see the prophet beginning to rationalize and relax — to become settled in his surroundings. Yahweh sends a second message. In keeping with our thoughts on the prophet's first call, we can suppose that the prophetic party had begun to reassert itself back in Samaria. Jeroboam was not overthrown, although opinions differed whether he was a "good" or "evil" king.[90] Even though some prophets had fled, the king chose not to make them scapegoats — preferring to point south to the damage to the Jerusalem temple and the judgment of Yahweh on Judah's king.[91] Thus the catastrophe began to be remembered as "Uzziah's earthquake." Affairs of state had to be resumed, and rumors of disquiet in Assyria made Jonah's mission all the more important. Yahweh and his king were to be served, "Arise, Jonah, and go!" The time was 762 or 761 BCE.

---

[88] See Chapter 3.

[89] H. Clay Trumbull, "Jonah in Nineveh," *Journal of Biblical Literature*: Vol. XI, Part I.

[90] This may account for the duality of outlook in II Kings 14:24 and 27.

[91] The *Books of Chronicles*, written from Judean sources, completely ignore Jeroboam II.

Sometime during this period, Jeroboam established control over the cities of Damascus and Hamath in north Syria (II Kings 14:28). Jonah is connected with this campaign by his prophecy of success. He may have been doing espionage during his stay in Phoenicia. If so, he could have posed as a horse-trader on the plains of Issus (or Kue).[92] There had been a group of Hebrew merchants in that region since Solomon's day. There is another interesting conjecture, and it is only that. We know from inscriptions that the king of Hamath was Zakir. This is a name of Semitic rather than Aramaic origin. He is described by Assyrians as a usurper — the son of a nobody. Hebrew tradition says that Jonah married the daughter of a certain Zechariah. It's tempting to suppose that Zakir was placed in power by Jeroboam and that his daughter was given to Jonah to seal Israel's control. The name Zechariah is so popular during this period as to make this a very uncertain identification. We do know that Zakir gained considerable influence throughout Syria at the same time that Jeroboam was extending his control there.

So Jonah forsook whatever respite he had found in Cilicia and traveled east to Nineveh. The overland distance from the north Phoenician coast to Nineveh is about 400 miles. As a caravan travels, this is a month's journey — Darius's pony express made it some years later in about a week. How then can the Bible claim that Nineveh was a city of three days' journey?

The Jerusalem Talmud solves the problem by claiming that Jonah was ejaculated from the fish a distance of "965 parasangs" — an uncertain Persian measure totaling over 2,000 miles — so that the prophet was within a three days' walk of the great city. (It would have required the first sub-orbital flight!)

The explanation was more scholarly when Austen H. Layard reported on his excavations at Nineveh in 1853:

> *If we take the four great mounds of Nimroud, Konijunjik, Khorsabad, and Karamles as the corners of the square it will be found that its four*

---

[92] In I Kings 10:28 read "Kue" for "and linen yarn." See J. A. Thompson, *The Bible and Archaeology*: 103.

> *sides correspond pretty accurately with the 480 stadia or 60 miles of the geographer.*[93]

In other words, Nineveh and its environs (though Sargon built Khorsabad after Jonah's time) formed a metropolis with a circumference of three days' journey on foot. Anxious to help, others have allowed Jonah three days to make a zigzag journey proclaiming doom through Nineveh's streets.[94]

It's evident that use of a day's journey as a measure of distance depends on the conveyance. A society on foot would interpret it differently from one accustomed to fast horses. A maritime civilization whose ships customarily traveled both day and night would outdistance one whose sailors sought the beach each evening. What did the Hebrew writer mean by a day's journey?

There are three distinct words for *journey* in Hebrew. The slowest pace, *naca,* pictures a donkey caravan. This word is derived from the root meaning *to pull up tent stakes.* Somewhat faster is a *darek* journey — the forced march of infantry and bowmen. In all save two instances the Bible uses one of these words. The exceptions are the references in Jonah and Nehemiah 2:6. There the word is *mahalek* whose root is *yalak,* to flow. In the latter reference it is clear that Nehemiah intends to make the initial stages of the trip back to Jerusalem by riverboat. We apply the same inference to Jonah's journey.

The ruins of Nineveh (positively identified by inscriptions on its paving bricks) lie on the Tigris river directly across from present-day Mosul. The Assyrians used the river as Main Street (as do their descendents today) and had developed their boating skills to a high degree. Since they traveled both day and night, a day's journey was about 40 miles in a current that flowed 2-3 miles per hour.[95]

The meaning of the text, then, is that Jonah revealed himself as a prophet and began to deliver his "one deep, brief cry of woe" at a point

---

[93] Austen Henry Layard,, *Nineveh and Its Remains* (New York: 1850), Vol. 2, 247.
[94] Some manuscripts exchange the commonly accepted version and allow 40 days for the trip and three days for Nineveh's repentance.
[95] Assyrians were so precise that they used different words for an upstream or a downstream journey.

about 120 river miles upstream of Nineveh. In the year 761 that point was precisely the frontier of Assyrian control.

Now that we have developed the Assyrian outpost as Jonah's destination, let us return to Phoenicia to reconstruct his trail. The overland route passed through Aleppo, Carchemish, Harran, Urfa (Edessa), Amedi (Diyarbakir), and Tille. To guard against the dangers of the road, Jonah undoubtedly joined a merchant caravan. A caravan was a highly organized affair with a commander and a contingent of mercenary soldiers. The entire caravan was on a contract basis, operating on a schedule with penalties for failure to pick up or deliver on time. Since this was before the days of coinage, letters of credit were used. The merchants as well as the soldiers were polyglot, drawn from the diverse cities along the route. As a practical necessity, their native tongue gave way to Aramaic, which became the commercial language of the Near East. The soldiers and merchant chiefs rode horseback or on white donkeys — a status symbol. Camels were used for the long hauls, and donkey caravans joined and left the main group at each city. It was not unusual for a caravan to include over 100 people and twice that number of animals.

Going eastward the cargo consisted of olive oil and wine, crimson and purple cloth and white linen, ivory and cedar work, as well as semi-refined copper, silver, and iron from the mines of Tarsus. Although camels can cover up to 100 miles a day, the pattern was about 50 miles between trade centers. This permitted traveling in the evening and early morning — days were spent encamped in perspiration and lethargy. The stopovers were several days at each city, so Jonah's trip from Phoenicia to the Tigris took at least the better part of a month.

Aleppo was at the crossroads of caravan routes. The road from the south through Hamath and Damascus joined the King's Highway and the Jordan valley. Most Phoenician goods went by ship or raft to ports like Karkar and then up the Orontes valley to Aleppo. Aleppo lay in a ring of rounded limestone hills, broken north and south by the Chalys (now Kuwaik) river. From ancient times the river has been used for irrigation, and Aleppo's gardens rivaled those of fabled Damascus. The name of the river means *milk* in Hebrew *(chalab)*. Abraham is said to have pastured his cattle here on the journey from Harran to Canaan.

We know little of its religious practices in the eighth century. Aleppo was a member of the Hittite confederacy and remained Hittite in outlook long after the confederacy's fall c. 1200. Assyria conquered the city (which they called *Halman*) in 853, and it remained tributary for the rest of the century. In Jonah's day it was probably part of an anti-Assyrian coalition headed by the northern kingdom of Urartu. It was not until 743 that Assyrian resurgence brought Aleppo back under their control.

A quarry of hard stone just north of the city supplied building materials, and there was a bitumen spring nearby. The seepage was traded for waterproofing boats.

The main road to the east soon split, the southern branch serving the Euphrates valley down past Babylon to the Bitter Sea (Persian Gulf). Jonah's caravan took the north route, which followed the river bank until it reached the ford at Carchemish.

Carchemish, now Jerablus, was an imposing city, and excavations prove its grandeur. Along the Euphrates' bank there is a great wall, beautifully fitted with black basalt slabs. At the shallows of the river, the wall is breached with a mammoth gate. Its inner walls and buttresses of basalt and limestone are carved in bas relief. From this water gate, a processional way used for state ceremonies leads to an acropolis. All along the avenue are carvings of foot soldiers, chariots with horses trampling the enemy, and archers downing those who flee. The last slab is of the fertility goddess Ishtar, posed holding her breasts. Up the hillside is a long flight of steps, leading to a temple door flanked with basalt lions. In the preeminent place are carvings of the Hittite trinity — headed by Chemosh, god of fire, who gave the city its name.

Harran is about an 18-hour caravan journey from Carchemish. The fertile plain surrounding the city was the first resting place of Terah and his son Abraham in the Biblical account of their western migration from Ur. The city was considered sacred by all Semitic peoples. The inhabitants honored the Moon god Sin as their special patron. Their worship included human sacrifice, particularly of blond or albino babies and white-haired old men — a connection to the Moon's silvery light.

Harran's religious practices were both complementary and antagonistic to the Sun cult of Asshur. Although Assyrians were anxious to propitiate whatever gods might exist, they could not afford to let a rival god gain ascendency. Each strong Assyrian king made concession to Harran's influence by permitting the city to retain a degree of autonomy, extracting whatever tribute circumstances dictated. There is no record of forced deportation of its citizens, a normal Assyrian practice for conquered peoples. No western expedition was even attempted until the princes of Harran were either mollified or pacified. Shalmaneser III (c. 850) went so far as to rebuild and enlarge the temple of Sin and called it "The Temple of Rejoicing."

As the lunar cult center, Harran had a prestige beyond its political power. This is illustrated by records of a desert city established by a feudal noble about this time. His city was only a short distance west of Asshur, yet he named it Dur Bel-Harran-bel-usar (May the Lord of Harran protect the lord of the city). Excavations reveal that the dedicatory incantations have no mention of the king of Assyria or of the great god Asshur. Such an affront could not have been lightly made.

Just a few hours' ride from Harran, in the northwest corner of the plain, is Urfa (Edessa). The present village is at the base of a limestone hill which contains ruins of the ancient citadel. It is a stony and naked country, and volcanic evidence abounds. Here is the spring, sacred to Atergatis, who is further honored with a pool of sacred fish. When Ainsworth's expedition visited the city in 1888, the inhabitants still worshipped the fish-god and left unmolested the 20,000 carp in the springs and the river Daisan (ancient Scirtus).[96]

We can wonder if and when Jonah revealed the story of his miraculous preservation to his caravan companions. If he did, the temptation to do so in the surroundings of Urfa would have been great. In any case, the worship of fish and of water would have renewed in the prophet the memory of his own experience.

---

[96] See Chapter 11 for more about Oannes. Ainsworth also connects the worship of the fish-god with Oannes. See William Francis Ainsworth, *A Personal Narrative of the Euphrates Expedition* (London: 1888).

Now the caravan left the plains behind and entered the mountain valleys that produced provincial clans every bit as warlike as the early Scots. Although the border moved with Assyrian military pressure, the basic allegiance of the clans was to the Vannic kingdom to the north. What measure of union that existed was brought to focus about 840 by Sarduris I who established his capital at Tuspas on the shores of Lake Van. The Assyrians called these people "the Urartu" (precursor of Ararat) or "children of Khaldis" (Chaldean) after their supreme god.

As the Hattic empire dissolved, the Vannic peoples gained control of the mines of the Taurus mountains and restricted Assyrian trade. Although Sarduris characterized himself as "king of the world, king of kings, king of the riverland," (*i.e.,* the Tigris-Euphrates plain), he was defeated in 831 by Shalmaneser III. The Assyrians established a series of frontier forts at Tille, Nasibina, Tushan, and Nairi to blockade the exits from the mountain passes.

The intervening kings of Van husbanded their strength and consolidated their northern hegemony, but the great grandson of Sarduris, Argistis I, turned to directly confront Assyrian might. He came to power in 785, and the sacred rock at Tuspas describes 14 successive military campaigns. Most of the wars of Shalmaneser IV were against Argistis.

By the time of Jonah, Argistis had control of the upper reaches of the Tigris and was making raids within a few miles of Nineveh.

As the caravan moved northeast from Urfa, skirting the mountains (around what is now Karaca Dag), it was under the watchful eyes of Vannic sentries. At their next stop, Amedi, there would be tribute and tolls to pay before the merchants could proceed. The trade was too lucrative for Argistis to blockade it entirely. Besides, the copper mines north of Amedi needed markets. Most of the metal went west to strengthen the Cappadocian coalition, but a trickle went south to Assyria at a good price.

Amedi (now Diyarbakir) was on the right bank of the upper Tigris, which flows in a deep, open valley. The appearance of the black, basaltic valley walls is depressing, but the ancient frontier village thrived on trade from the Euxine coast as well as from Phoenicia.[97] Although most caravans continued overland, it was possible to unload cargo on rafts of logs or into skin boats for downriver ports. However, during the spring floods, the current between Amedi and Tille was treacherous, and in other seasons the upper river was shallow.

Amedi did not enjoy the same tolerance from the Assyrians as the cities of the Harranian plain. Rather, as a frontier village, it was used as an example of the futility of resistance to the Assyrian army. In 867 Ashur-nasir-apal II tells of heads staked as high as the city gate and of captives impaled round about the walls — scarcely a program to instill love and loyalty among its citizens.[98]

Assyrian *limmu* lists[99] reveal that in 800 Amedi's governor, one Marduk-Shemani, acted for King Adad-Nirari while the army attacked the forces of Argistis in Media.

In 763 the nominal governor was named Tab-bel. He follows other western governors in the *limmu* cycle — which suggests political necessity rather than chance. By this time Argistis controlled the surrounding countryside. Assyrian power was concentrated in its walled cities.

The overland route continued along the south bank of the Tigris past the store-city of Tushan, noted as a grain center. The straw of the fields in the area was particularly good for making mud bricks. In 885 Ashur-nasir-apal I built a palace in Tushan in testimony to his control of the upper river. The trade route went along the river bank to a point opposite Tille, a frontier post like Amedi. Tille guarded the pass where the Bitlis Chai (now Pesh Khabur) joins the upper Tigris to form a

---

[97] Perhaps Josephus's source picked up Jonah's journey at this point and was unable to decide which road was the one Jonah traveled.

[98] This may have been the genesis of the Arabic proverb, "In Amedi there are black stones, black dogs, and black hearts."

[99] Tablets of Assyrian eponyms are practically complete from the 12th century to the end of the empire. The practice was to name each year for the official *(limmu)* who was titular head of government when the king was in the field with the army. Duties appear to have been principally ceremonial and religious. The first eponym in a cycle was the king's, followed by cabinet officials. If the king still reigned after his principal officials had served, the succession went to lesser governors by lot.

navigable stream. Here the overland route ended for large cargo, and rafts or boats were loaded for the remainder of the journey. Here, too, massive cedar beams from the mountains were lashed together and floated downstream for temple construction. The entire lower Tigris valley depended on this river transportation. Here, we may surmise, Jonah left the caravan. The direct distance to Nineveh is 68 miles, but 120 miles by river. Nineveh was three days' journey from Tille.

The governor of Tille at this time was probably Mushallim-nimib. We meet him first in 793 in the year of his eponym. He still held office for the next cycle in 766. Assyrian control was shaky, however, as a stele halfway between Tille and Nineveh attests. The monument bears witness to a battle between Argistis and the Assyrian army and mentions Mushallim. So audacious had the armies of Urartu become.

Although the basic confrontation in the area during this period was between Assyria and Urartu, there were many vassal states that wanted to take advantage of Assyria's relative weakness. Dissident governors seized the opportunity to assert their independence. One who merits our attention is Apliya. He enters the *limmu* lists as governor of Mazamua, an eastern province, in 768. Shalmaneser IV and his field marshal, Shamshi-ilu, had kept continuous pressure on Urartu and even attacked Damascus and Hazrek in 774-773. Shalmaneser died suddenly in the field, possibly from the plague. When his son Asshur-Dan succeeded him, the armies, still under the control of Shamshi-ilu, attacked south toward Babylon in the territories of Gananati and Marad. Mazamua was the natural headquarters for this operation, and its governor appears to have found favor with the young king.

During Apliya's eponym year, the king and the army were "in the country," a sure sign of unrest. The year Apliya spent in Kalah, the capital city, he put to his own use, increasing his power. Encouraged by Argistis' military prowess and the evident disfavor of the gods towards Shamshi-ilu, Apliya reappeared in 763 as the leader of a rebellion. Asshur, the former capital and Shamshi-ilu's home town, was the first to revolt. Arappha, another of the great cities the central triangle,[100]

---

[100] The area around the junction of the Tigris and the Upper Zab rivers included Assyria's principal cities.

joined the revolution. Apliya next appeared fomenting rebellion in the western provinces of Amedi and Guzana. Even though the omens are against him, Shamshi-ilu survived[101] and stayed as *turtanu* when Ashur-Nirari IV came to the throne in 753. Apliya disappeared from Assyrian records, but we shall have occasion to study his career more closely. Jonah at Tille was in the heart of the rebellion, and his link to Apliya is more than contemporary.

---

[101] "Him that holdeth the Sceptre in the house of Eden" (*i.e.,* the city of Bit-Adini) in Amos 1 may be a reference to Shamshi-ilu as the real power behind the weak kings.

10 Why Were the Ninevites Repentant?

Conditions in Nineveh

"In what hour will the city be destroyed?
In what watch will it come upon us,
The sound of the dreadful earthquake?"
They thought that the city would fall at even —
The evening came and yet it stood;
They thought they should be swallowed up at night —
That night they continued among the living;
The twilight passed and they were not destroyed;
They thought the city would fall in the morning —
The morning came and their hope increased.
At the season when they expected to be no more,
Suddenly salvation was theirs!
    - Part VII, 9, 12-17, 18-23

Professor T. K. Cheyne, writing of the miracles in the *Book of Jonah*, said:

> *The greatest of the improbabilities is a moral one; can we conceive of a large heathen city being converted by an obscure foreign prophet?*[102]

The purpose of this chapter is to show that Jonah cannot be described as "obscure" and that, given the circumstances of 761 BCE, the "conversion" of Nineveh was not an improbable result of his mission.

We left the prophet saying goodbye to the caravan at Tille. This city was more than a frontier town. Situated at the confluence of the tributaries which together make the sacred Tigris, the town was devoted to Ea, the water god, and a pantheon of lesser sons, daughters, and consorts of the great god. Even such strong kings as Tiglath Pileser I and Shalmaneser III made pilgrimages to Mount Nal, near Tille, where the headwaters of the lower Tigris emerge from a subterranean cavern. The cave is a wonderland of stalactites and stalagmites, and

---

[102] Quoted in John Kennedy, *On the Book of Jonah, a Monograph* (London: 1895): 43.

rock-cut stairs lead to terraces on the summit where the Assyrians probably built a temple. Inscriptions invoking the favor of the gods abound on the sheer cliffs. Although the Assyrians worshipped the Sun as a symbol of their military might, the common people identified themselves more closely with the sacred river and its god. In much the same way as the Hebrews regarded themselves as Yahweh's vineyard, Assyrians looked upon their nation as Ea's channel:

> *O Stream, thou who has created all things!*
> *When the great gods dug thee out*
> *They set grace upon thy banks;*
> *In thee has Ea, king of the deeps, established his dwelling.*
> *They gave thee a flood comparable to none other!*
> *Fire and wrath, splendor and terror,*
> *Have Ea and Marduk bestowed upon thee,*
> *Thou judgest the cause of Mankind.*
> *Mighty Stream!*
> *Exalted Stream!*
> *Righteous Stream!*[103]

Ea was patron of irrigation and thus god of wisdom and of all skills. The mythology surrounding him clearly casts him in the role of mankind's savior and advocate. He was responsible for all healing. In the Ea-ritual for sickness, the priest washed the patient in water from the sacred river. An image of the demon causing the sickness was placed in a tiny boat and let go in the Tigris. As it sank into the water or was carried out of sight, the illness departed.

The marvelous effect of Jonah's preaching becomes more explicable in the light of this worship of the water god. Surely the initial Assyrian reaction to the story of salvation from the watery abyss would be to credit the powers of Ea. Did Jonah recognize this effect and use it to advantage? The Biblical account gives a hint that he did. Up to the time of Jonah's Assyrian preaching, all the prophet's dealings have been with Yahweh (translated "The Lord" in the King James Version). Now, suddenly, the appeal is not from The Lord, but from The Great God

---

[103] Quoted in Society of Biblical Literature, *Journal of Biblical Literature* (1929): Vols. 48-49, 174.

El. Both Yahweh and El are found throughout the Old Testament, and scholars have given much study to the uses of each word. El is especially connected to the nomadic tradition, and Yahweh is revealed in the more provincial covenant tradition. El appears as a divine appellation in Moab and south Arabia as well as in Hittite and associated Syrian cultures. Use of that name would be recognized as a universalist appeal throughout the ancient Near East.

We need not fault Jonah as needlessly compromising his message by this approach. The "Billy Sunday of Nineveh" started where his audience was. Eight centuries later, St. Paul the evangelist was to begin from a similar base as he preached Jesus Christ to the Athenians as the revelation of the Unknown God they already worshipped.

The eclipse that served as a text for Amos's dire warnings did not go unnoticed in Nineveh. In fact the great historian Dr. A. T. Olmstead says the effect was so ominous as to be the immediate cause for the revolt of 763-751. The *limmu* list inscribes the most important event of the year:

> *Bur (ilu)-sagale of the city of Guzana (limmu). A revolt in the City of Asshur. In the month of Sivan an eclipse of the Sun took place.* [104]

Directly underneath is a horizontal mark to separate this calamitous news from the rest of the inscription.

Of course, the Assyrians used celestial movements as one of their chief omen sources. Together with the Babylonians, they were heirs to the Sumerian division of the heavens into precincts that became identified with certain gods — signs of the zodiac. The movements of the planet "wanderers" had special significance. Astrology reached its dramatic zenith in the divination of a spectacular eclipse. Both the Sun and the Moon were divided into quadrants assigned to various sections of the land — and woe to that province on which the shadow fell. The Assyrian priests could follow the relatively short lunar eclipse cycle and knew that the Moon in eclipse appears at six-month intervals for 2 - 2.5 years, followed by 17 lunations with no eclipses.[105] Such information was held secret to enhance priestly power. Solar eclipses, particularly

---

[104] Quoted in Rogers, *Op. cit.*: 233.
[105] The Greeks based their calendar on this Metonic cycle.

total, are so infrequent at any given spot as to make prediction difficult. Certainly the technique was unknown in the ninth century. Although the explanations are couched in mythological terms, the priests were aware that a solar eclipse is caused by interference of the Moon — but this fact made the event even more ominous.

It is difficult to reconstruct the exact meaning that the astrologers would give to the eclipse of June 15, 763 BCE. [106] There was some latitude for political expediency. However, the divination, of necessity, contained certain recognizable standard elements to make it plausible to the people. One inescapable conclusion of a total eclipse was that calamity was to overtake *all* Assyria — no province would escape if the warning went unheeded. The second fact is that the Moon held ascendancy over the Sun. In terms of the times, the lunar cults of the western provinces could take heart as the cities of the triangle under the Sun-disk of Shamesh-Asshur went into eclipse. The accent on the old east-west split was food indeed for revolution. Various luminaries in the hierarchy would be singled out and their destinies judged by the position of their natal planets. We can imagine how Shamshi-ilu (the Sun is my god) must have reacted. The young Asshur-Dan (Asshur is my fortune) trembled at the word. The time was ripe for Apliya to incite the city of Asshur to revolt to escape their otherwise certain fate. The western provinces were not long in joining the rebellion.

---

[106] Modern star charts, extrapolated back to this date, indicate star positions that were very ominous. Jupiter, sacred to Marduk, was in superior conjunction on June 12 and had disappeared into the light of the Sun for a period of about 40 days. Mercury (Nabu) reached conjunction on June 16. Venus (Ishtar) gained greatest westward elongation on June 22 and started to move toward the Sun, growing brighter until August 1, about 40 days from the eclipse. Saturn was moving toward the Sun and disappeared in conjunction by mid-July. Mars alone (Nergal, god of the netherworld) was able to withstand the pull of the Sun and to begin to move away starting about July 22. Assyrian priests were able to predict these apparent planetary movements. Not only did the Sun and the Moon disappear during the eclipse, but also four of the five major planets were not visible or seemed to be drawn into the cosmic whirlpool. This may be responsible for the strange statements in Joel 2:10 and 3:15 and Amos 5:18, 20 and 8:9 that even the stars will be dark in the Day of Yahweh. Normally, of course, the stars would shine more brightly during an eclipse.

Into this unrest came Jonah with a message of hope. Even though he appeared in Nineveh some time after the eclipse, it was still fresh in everyone's memory. The Ninevites regarded the eclipse as "the beginning of troubles" — they had been under a curse ever since. Jonah had seen the same eclipse, had experienced the terrible judgment of his God which followed, but he had been saved and preserved so that Ea-El could again save his children. So even in the hubbub of the times, Jonah was not likely to go unnoticed.

Now Ea and his associated deities definitely have lunar character — though not so outright as the god Sin. Ea's festival was at the autumnal equinox when the Sun's power is at the wane. His symbol is the goat-fish of Capricorn, of lunar derivation. Ea's roots are also deep in Sumerian tradition, where Enki was his antecedent. All in all, any promotion of the water god at this time would have appealed to the Assyrian mind as having that neat blend of tradition and expediency that would satisfy the omen without suffering its consequences.

But what of Jonah's message, "Yet forty days and Nineveh shall be overthrown"? Did the prophet expect an earthquake like the one that wrecked Samaria, Jerusalem, and the surrounding lands? As illustrated by the quotation beginning this chapter, local tradition from early times is that the city was continually shocked throughout the period of Jonah's preaching. It is doubtful if Jonah would have couched his warning in terms so specific as to permit no other interpretation. As far as the rulers were concerned, the revolution was the clear and present danger, and the prophet's words would be fulfilled if the revolt were a success.

Why the 40-day grace? We have already mentioned that occluded planets disappear for about this length of time in the zodiacal glare of the Sun. Thus a new horoscope was possible only after this time. There are many examples in Near Eastern texts of omens effective for a 40-day period. There is another facet that the Ninevites would appreciate — 40 is the number sacred to Ea. The Assyrians used combination sexagesimal-decimal numbering, and the supreme father-god Anu was assigned the number 60 as perfection. Ea was also known as *Shanabi*, god of two-thirds (40/60) — more of the perfect 60 later.

"And Jonah began to enter the city a days' journey." We can visualize a religious procession taking shape at Tille. Jonah's boat may have contained no idol, but those recent hearers who believed enough of his message to make the pilgrimage would not leave Ea behind. Perhaps there were shaven priests wearing fish-head masks, like those pictured in the bas reliefs at Khorsabad. Interestingly, Jewish tradition says that Jonah lost all his hair in the fish's belly — or did he remove it in deference to his hosts? Perhaps the gilded ceremonial boats, usually saved for the annual pilgrimage of Ea, were borne from the temple precincts garlanded with flowers. Assyrian gods were no stay-at-homes to be shut off in a dark holy-of-holies. They went to battle and on the hunt — their barges were a part of each festival as the gods were transported from their *bit akitu* house outside the city walls to their particular temples.

After the river procession had proceeded downstream one day's journey, Jonah called a halt. Here at the two-thirds point (shades of Ea) was another shrine. You can still see the site today beneath the peak of Judi Dagh — the mountain where the natives say Ut-napishtim's ark grounded as Ea saved him from the worldwide flood.[107] Jonah could have taken his text from Noah and hammered home that El and Ea were similar in their concern for mankind. There was salvation even after 40 days and 40 nights (that number again) of judgment.

Here is the narrowest part of the Tigris, now known as the Baghloja defile, scarcely 40 feet wide. Rock ledges and boulders make navigation difficult, even by raft. The overlaid trail winds along on the south bank and makes no crossing.

The character of the river changes as it nears Nineveh. The deep gorges and swift currents give way to mere tranquil flow over a broad, shingly bed. The fish spawn here, and the natives still give holy respect to the shale bars. At Nineveh was the main road crossing linking the cities of the triangle to the western trading posts. There were probably settlements on both banks.

---

[107] The designation of the more lofty Mt. Ararat further north is a rather recent development and may be considered a concession to rational Western minds, who might expect the ark to settle on the highest point after the Flood.

Although it justified the Biblical term of *great city,* Nineveh was not the chief city of Assyria at this time. The seat of government had been at Kalah since 860. It was not until 700, when Sennacherib decided to make Nineveh his capital, that the city became synonymous with Assyrian power. Sennacherib's descriptions of the narrow, crooked streets and the broken temples he rebuilt are probably overly severe, but it is true that in the absence of booty that flowed in with conquest, most Ninevites must have lived at the bare subsistence level in unadorned surroundings.

Asshur was known as a priest-ridden city, Kalah for it bureaucracy. Nineveh was controlled by the military and even to Assyrian historians, its people were a quarrelsome sort. This seems to have led to some restrictions against bearing arms within the city. Esarhaddon (c. 675) mentions this long-standing taboo as he complains that revolutionaries actually fought within the city, "which is a godless thing to do."

We cannot be sure of the size of the city before it became the capital. At its greatest extent, the walls of the city were about a six-mile circuit enclosing about 1,850 acres. Dr. George Rawlinson's studies reveal a population density in Assyrian cities of not more than 100 persons per acre, allowing for streets, open squares, gardens, and temples. Thus in its heyday the population within the walls was about 175,900 and was undoubtedly less in Jonah's day.[108]

As befits an army town, Nineveh's patroness was Ishtar, goddess of fertility and war. However, Assyrians seem to have been less licentious in their worship than either Babylonians or Hittites. Ritual prostitution was accepted, but participation was limited to the priesthood and the general populace had no orgiastic rites. There seems to have been some ethical revival under young Adad-Nirari and his mother-regent Sammuramat. Long-forgotten Nabu, god of ancient Borsippa, begins to appear again in compound names. Some find a hint of monotheism in the image of Nabu erected at Kalah and its inscription, "Thou who shall follow after, trust in Nabu, trust not in any other god." The Nabu temple at Nineveh was restored in 787, but as soon as Adad-Nirari

---

[108] Population estimates based on Jonah 4:11 must be discounted. See Chapter 11.

could act on his own, he appears to have given the reform no support. Actually, the movement might better be described as henotheistic[109] since the various priestly cults were in constant struggle to elevate their particular patron. One text depicts all the gods as priests of Ninurta:

> *Enlil and Ninlil are his eyes,*
> *Sin is the pupil of his eyes,*
> *Anu and Antu are his lips,*
> *The Seven Divine Beings are his teeth*
> *His breast is Nabu.*[110]

It is extremely improbable that the Nabu revival contributed much toward acceptance of Jonah's message. The religious climate of Nineveh could best be described as tepid.

> *So the people of Nineveh believed El, and proclaimed a fast, and put on sackcloth, from the greatest of them even to the least of them (Jonah 3:5).*

The Ninevites believed — some of them out of fear of the omen of the eclipse, some out of fear of the power of Urartu and the revolution that seethed up to the city's walls, some out of wonder at the experiences of the prophet. We need not suppose an ethical reform in this instance. By Assyrian standards, the anxiety was to find a formula to propitiate the gods. By Hebrew standards, Jonah was intent on achieving for Jeroboam the political influence that would be Israel's salvation. For the prophet, God's work and Hebrew survival were so inextricably bound together that what served one, served the other.

The ceremony of fasting and putting on sackcloth and ashes was not at all alien to Assyria.[111] We think of the custom as uniquely Hebrew,[112] but it goes back to Sumerian civilization and beyond. We have already seen[113] that it was part of "The Descent of Inanna to the Netherworld." Assyrian literature is replete with similar references. In all cases the

---

[109] worshipping one god while not denying others exist

[110] Quoted in Georges Contenau, *Everyday Life in Babylon and Assyria* (1954): 262.

[111] Although the custom of covering head and body with dust must have been especially abhorrent to societies practicing ritual ablutions.

[112] The Assyrian reaction was an echo of the Hebrew penance after the great earthquake as described in Amos 8:10.

[113] See Chapter 8.

context is death or salvation from it. The inhabitants of the netherworld, where "dust lay on door and bolt," had only dust and ashes to eat and went about naked. The use of sackcloth also has the connotation of disguise, since the night-demon of death would scarcely bother one of such low station.

Soon the demonstration surrounding Jonah raised such a clamor that the ruler of the city heard of it. A messenger summoned Jonah to the palace to explain. No doubt the *malek* saw in the prophet yet another soothsayer with a formula to overcome the evil omens. With the threat of revolution coming ever closer to Nineveh itself, anyone with a public following must be heard. Jonah repeated the message, "Yet forty days and Nineveh will be overthrown." The ruler had the pragmatism of one accustomed to multiple gods and their vacillations. "Who can tell if El will turn and repent and turn away from his fierce anger, that we perish not?" He issued a proclamation to be heralded in the streets. He joined his people in following the formula of humiliation. His actions were entirely consistent with rituals prescribed in Assyrian omen texts.

Just to protect himself from everyday demons, the ruler used a throne and footstool set on pointed cones — to narrow the path from the netherworld below. Visitors entered the palace through a hallway with multiple turns. If, in spite of precautions, the night hag's children threatened the ruler, they could still be misdirected. The king might find a substitute, *puhu*, for the throne. Sometimes if he "laid aside his robe from him" (ritual abdication for a season) it would be sufficient. In more ominous circumstances, a statue or even a human slave was arrayed in the trappings of office to receive the vengeance of the gods. One of the omen texts relates:

> *If during an eclipse the planet Jupiter can be seen, it means safety for the king: but instead of him someone, great or humble, shall die.*[114]

Cases are reported where the *baru* (diviner) or *ashipu* (exorcist) was encouraged, presumably by the king, to perform ritual murder so the king could resume government. There seems to be little conscience involved — the god's will must be carried out even if human help is needed.

---

[114] Quoted in Contenau, *Op.cit.*: 298.

The wording of the royal proclamation deserves attention: "Let everyone turn from his evil way and from the violence that is in their hands." The Hebrew word for violence (*hammas*) has an Assyro-Babylonian equivalent (*immasu*) that is translated *clamor* in certain texts, such as the Flood Epic:

> *Enlil heard their clamor and said to the great gods: "Oppressive has become the clamor of mankind, by their clamor they prevent sleep."*[115]

The Assyrian words for sin (*hatu*) and shout (*hadu*) hint that any noise other than a priestly chant was an affront to the gods.[116] The decree was a plea to the mob to cease its hubbub and incipient rebellion rather than a request for repentance and ethical behavior.

The ruler made the cattle a part of the ritual humiliation. Why? Although there are no direct accounts of similar instances in cuneiform texts,[117] the action is consistent with the Assyrian attitude toward animals. Most flocks and herds of substantial size belonged to temples. Their ears were marked with the symbol of the divinity who owned them — Asshur's Sun-disk, Ishtar's star, the scribal wedge of Nabu, or the crescent of Sin. Such animals were watched closely for omens, and any sickness or blemish would be promptly interpreted. Even their behavior under special circumstances (as when refusing to enter the gate of a city) could have evil portent.

Before the history of the Assyrian nation became known through archaeological study, scholars universally scoffed at the Biblical phrase "the King of Nineveh." It was like calling the British monarch "the King of London" at the height of the Empire. Now that the record is known, the Biblical writer is startlingly correct. The Assyrian king's control in 761 included only Nineveh and Kalah as major cities — an area scarcely 100 miles in diameter. Perhaps it was actually Asshur-Dan

---

[115] Pritchard, *Op. cit.*: 106.

[116] Bronze bells and gongs have been recovered that were used to drive out demons — the antithesis of our ideas about worship. The motif of the fish-god is prominent in decoration of these articles.

[117] However, Herotodus reports that Persian animals joined their owners in mourning several centuries later during the campaign against Greece. Metsudath David says that animals had no need of repentance, but withholding their food was an added penance for their owners.

III whom Jonah confronted. The word *malek* could have been equally applied to Shamshi-ilu, since he governed the army headquartered at Nineveh. Or it could have been ascribed to Ninib-mukin-akhe, the governor of Nineveh who was also *limmu* during those dark days. In any case, the Biblical account is corroborated by Assyrian history:

> *And El saw their works, that they turned from their evil way; and El repented of the evil, that he said he would do unto them; and he did it not (Jonah 3:10).*

11 Doest Thou Well to Be Angry?

Revived Diplomacy

> Where is thy justice, O Jonah?
> Dost thou compare the city with the gourd?
> Thy kindness is toward the bower,
> Thy cruelty toward the city.
> The gourd which is given for food is more to thee than the
> eaters;
> The gourd, made to decay,
> Is preferred by thee to penitents.
> Thou thinkest the leaves of the gourd
> Are better than rational men;
> The blossoms and flowers of a gourd,
> Than children and young persons!
>   - Part VII, 180-191

The next picture is of Jonah alone in a garden on the east side of
Nineveh. His only shelter is a booth of sticks. In the time of
Sennacherib, a park devoted to the god Nergel was at the east gate. It
was located "before the old bridge, by the Royal Road and the (Khosr)
river." In 700 BCE it was 50 *imers* in size — a plot equivalent to a field
requiring 120 bushels of grain to seed. Undoubtedly the park was old
when Sennacherib improved it, and it must have been there in Jonah's
time.

One would think that a seer who had produced the apotropaion[118] that
had saved a city would be popular — a guest in the palace or at least in
a noble house. Not so! The Assyrian fear of the demon world
permitted no communion with one who bore such charisma. The text
for ritual purity questioned the penitent:

---

[118] spell to ward off evil

> *Whether he has been is the company of a man under a spell, or slept in his bed, or sat upon his seat or eaten from his plate, or drunk from his cup?*[119]

Jonah fears for his life. He asks Yahweh (no longer El) to slay him, lest in the ebb and flow of the contending groups in Nineveh he be blamed for some mischance and flayed and skinned alive. Jonah is not at all sure at this point that the commotion he has aroused will redound to Israel's gain.

The verses that follow are graphic and colorful, but seem almost an anticlimax. Although Jonah had surely built many tabernacles *(Cukkoth)* to shield him from the Sun in the fields of Gath-Hepher, the booth in the Ninevite garden is not sufficient shelter. Yahweh causes a gourd to come up, literally "the son of the night," to give shade. The plant perishes just as quickly when a worm devastates it. Then the prophet must undergo the trial of a searing east wind. It is no wonder he faints and cries, "It is better for me to die than to live!"

Any Bible commentary will expound the moral teachings of this parable — for such it is. But our goal is to see if it has any meaning in history. In the interest of verisimilitude, some have identified the gourd as the *Palma Christi*, a variety of castor bean, and questioned whether it could grow up overnight without divine intervention. The worm[120] is variously thought of as the crimson-dye-yielding *coccus ilicus* (although the castor been is safe from this species)[121] or, in Professor J. S. Boyd's view, the black caterpillar, which "on warm days, when a small rain falls [is] generated in great numbers on this plant, which in one night, so often and so suddenly cut off its leaves that only their ribs remain."

Conservative John Calvin becomes almost naturalistic when explaining the miracle of the gourd:

> *We know that God, when he does anything beyond the (ordinary) course of nature, does, nevertheless, come near to nature in His working; He does outdo the (usual) course of nature, and yet does not desert it altogether ... In this case I do not doubt that God chose a plant which would quickly*

---

[119] See Jorgen Laessoe, *Studies on the Assyrian Ritual Series Bit Rimki* (1955).
[120] Hebrew *tola'ath*, also the word for *scarlet*.
[121] This species is found in arid country, as several varieties of cactus.

grow up even to such a height as this, and yet, that he surpassed the
wonted course of nature (by causing it to come up and to perish in a
night).[122]

The perils of the sirocco and of the mud gas formed when that east
wind blasts across the desert are well known. But other people have
faced it and survived. It was probably not much of a threat to Jonah's
life with the walls of Nineveh and the waters of the Khosr hard by.

Are we therefore to dismiss the parable as mere poetic hyperbole with
its components hazily identified? No, this story may well have a stricter
historical interpretation than has been previously suspected. The clue is
in the gourd — the protection that was, in literal Hebrew "the son of
the night." The gourd symbolizes a man — a man in whose shade
Jonah found protection. Who but the revolutionary Apliya whom we
met in Chapter 9? The connection is clearer if we analyze the Assyrian
equivalent for the unusual expression "the son of the night" — *apu-lilu.*
We are dealing with a pun on the rebel's name. Further, the word for
night and for *demon*[123] are the same. The pun literally becomes a curse. It
is exactly the epithet Ninevites would give a usurper who challenged
the king's power.

Let us now reconstruct the parable along historical lines. When Jonah
first entered Assyria, he was impressed by the power of Apliya in the
western provinces and felt that Yahweh's cause could best be served by
encouraging the rebellion. Apliya was the one who could protect Israel
(symbolized by the tabernacle) from the Sun-power of Asshur. But
history had a different fate for Apliya. His armies were defeated, not so
much by the hosts of Shamshi-ilu as they were by the worm of
pestilence — a sure sign of the disfavor of Nergal. Apliya himself most
likely died of the plague in 759, and the revolt was crushed completely
the next year. Jonah now was buffeted by the winds of rumor as

---

[122] Quoted in Thomas Thomason Perowne, *Obadiah and Jonah* (London: 1891):
87.
[123] Lilith was the female demon who roamed the night, especially attacking
children in desolate places. She remained in demonology through the Middle
Ages as a witch and is introduced as such in Goethe's *Faust.*

Shamshi-ilu regained control.[124] Perhaps Assyria would grow strong enough to attack farther west, even to Jeroboam's extended borders. Jonah would as soon die.

Yahweh reminds Jonah that the prophet had little to do with either the rise or fall of "the son of the night" and that Israel's influence rested with the "more than six-score thousand persons (Ninevites) that cannot discern between their right hand and their left hand." Most commentators interpret this phrase as being idiomatic for children. Such a translation is anachronistic and reflects neither Hebrew or Assyrian thinking of the time. There is no equivalence of childhood and innocence in the Old Testament or in cuneiform texts. In both societies, the youngsters were disciplined and otherwise ignored. An interpretation closer to Assyrian texts would regard the reference as to the uninitiated, *i.e.*, the common people, outside the noble and priestly classes.[125]

Another chain of logic leads to the same group in a different manner. The words for right and left hand are the same as for the directions north and south, since the Semite faced east as primal point. Thus, the allusion may be to those who have not taken sides in the rebellion backed by northern Urartu. Perhaps Yahweh spoke through the prophetic council back in Israel. That would be sufficient reason for speaking in symbolic terms in case the messenger or the message were intercepted. Yahweh is telling his prophet that the way to keep the Assyrian army at home is to appeal to the commoner's desire for peace. The nobles and priests backed the war machine, but the conscription of peasants alienated the lower classes. In fact, Assyrian power was not fully revived until Tiglath Pileser III,[126] several generations later,

---

[124] The idea that words without meaning are as hot winds is ancient. Talmudists emphasize that Jonah's words were "as wind, and no evil befell the people." The prophet became the laughingstock of Nineveh.

[125] A formula for Assyrian teachers of young priests is but one example of such usage: "The rites you perform may be seen by the pupil, but not by any stranger who is not versed in the oracles, or his days shall be numbered. The initiate may declare himself to the initiate. But those not initiated shall not behold the rites. That would be an abomination in the eyes of the great gods Anu, Enlil, and Ea."

[126] The "Pul" of II Kings 15:19.

abandoned the military draft and returned to professional soldiery to
rebuild the army.

In any Assyrian document, large numbers bear investigation of their
possible symbolic meanings.[127] The six-score thousand of the Bible
suggests a sexagesimal derivation. The Hebrew God is proclaiming
ascendency over Asshur's gods and their perfect number, 3,600 (60
times 60). Such a symbolic meaning is more important than numerical
accuracy. Any use of the number to estimate Nineveh's population is
doomed to failure and is but an exercise for a literal Western mind.

The Bible chronicler leaves the fainting Jonah under the withered gourd
eastward in Nineveh's garden. There is a later Babylonian account,
however, that scholars have suggested is related to the story of Jonah.
This account, by Babylonian priest Berossus who lived about 400 BCE,
is not preserved in the original. However, there are fragments quoted in
several Greek writings. Berossus may have been a Hebrew captive since
his name means *son of Hosea*. The Greek writers tell his story of the
appearance of several avatars of the fish-god. At the very beginning of
civilization, a personage, part man and part fish, came from the sea to
teach human beings the arts and crafts. Apollodorus passes on the
tradition that:

> ... *the whole body of the animal was like that of a fish; and had under a*
> *fish's head another head, and also feet below, similar to those of a man,*
> *subjoined to the fish's tail. His voice, too, and language were articulate and*
> *human; and a representation of him is preserved even to this day. This*
> *being used to converse with men in the day time, but took no food at that*
> *season; and he gave them an insight into letters, and sciences and every*
> *kind of art. He taught them to construct houses, to found temples, to*
> *compile laws, and explained to them the principles of geometrical*
> *knowledge. He made them to distinguish the seeds of earth, and showed*
> *them how to collect fruits. In short, he instructed them in everything which*
> *could tend to soften manners and to humanize mankind. From that time,*
> *so universal were his instructions, nothing material has been added by way*
> *of improvement. When the sun set, it was the custom of this being to*

---

[127] Sargon says of his palace in Khorsabad, "I built the circuit of the wall
16,283 cubits, the number of my name."

*plunge again into the sea, and abide all night in the deep, for he was
amphibious.*[128]

Berossus is quoted as saying that there were periodic reincarnations of
this great teacher. Each such messenger bore a new name: Oannes,
Euahanes, Annedotus, Odakon, Eneugamos, or Anementos.

When cuneiform texts began to be deciphered late in the 19th century,
there was much anticipation that there would be references to these
godly messengers, since classical writers mentioned them so
prominently. Although Dagon the fish-god and Ea the water god
appeared many times in the texts, there was no allusion to the tradition
ascribed to Berossus. None of the men-fish are mentioned.

As early as 1837, Professor F. C. Baur had attempted to relate Oannes
and Jonah. One formidable problem was that Oannes was connected
with the beginnings of civilization, and no one claimed such great
antiquity for Jonah. In 1892, Dr. H. Clay Trumbull, after deriving the
word *Jonah* from *Oannes* through Greek etymology, postulated that
Berossus, writing several centuries after the events, equated Jonah with
"the primal divinity of Nineveh" — then undiscovered.

This theory aroused little enthusiasm among Assyrologists. It remained
an open question until 1963, when Drs. W. W. Hallo and W. G.
Lambert, working independently, brought growing knowledge of
Assyro-Babylonian texts to bear and placed the Berossus tradition into
what must be very nearly its final context. Most of Berossus'
incarnation names are shown to be incipits[129] of myths in the Adapa
(the Babylonian Adam) cycle and not individual demigods at all. The
classical writers misinterpreted a list of Babylonian sacred writings —
there are 16 similar and more-ancient catalogs extant. Hallo concludes:

> *In sum, it would not be surprising if all the apkallu names turned out
> eventually to identify known cuneiform series. This would vindicate the
> long-held view of classical scholars that in Berossus' version of them they
> are none else than the revealed writings of the Babylonians. The excerpts of*

---

[128] Quoted in Fletcher S. Bassett, *Legends and Superstitions of the Sea and Sailors in
All Lands* (Chicago: 1885): 55.
[129] opening line of a text, such as a poem

Berossus preserved by later historians may be regarded in a sense as the last of the Sumerian literary catalogs.[130]

Lambert goes on to demonstrate that Oannes is the equivalent of the Sumerian phrase *recovered from the water* — the opening words of a sacred book. Granted that the earlier connection between Oannes and Jonah is correct, we must now admit the possibility that the name Jonah is derived from the Assyrian equivalent of Oannes (Eu-hanna) and not the other way around. What would be more natural then for the Assyrians to name the prophet "recovered from the water"? The connection of the sacred book to Enki (later Ea), the water god, reinforces our view that Jonah depended on the Ea tradition to give his message greater impact. Unless we wish to postulate an unnecessary coincidence, the equation of Jonah with *dove* must be abandoned along with the allegories that we have shown to be more readily explained by a direct interpretation.[131]

---

[130] William W. Hallo, *The World's Oldest Literature: Studies in Sumerian Belles Lettres* (Leiden: 2010): 150.

[131] There are also implications regarding Amittai.

12 Were There Further Adventures?

Final Days and Burial

> He went up, being renowned,
> And all men went forth to meet him,
> Kings trembled at his presence,
> Because he was the mighty preacher;
> They met him with great honor,
> From fear at his preaching.
> Each city which saw him grew pale,
> Lest he should enter and overturn it.
> Thus he was honored in the cities.
> Nineveh became an example;
> She was a mirror to the world
> In which justice might be viewed.
>   - Part VIII, 101, 102, 104-113

Granted the rather abrupt end to the Old Testament narrative, did Jonah continue to serve Israel as a prophet-diplomat? Jewish tradition says he did and details several missions with Jerusalem (not Samaria or Bethel) as headquarters. Jonah's wife, in particular, made repeated pilgrimages to the temple. But these stories seem a too-patent attempt to bestow orthodoxy on the truant prophet to be taken historically.

Spurred by the reference in II Kings 14:25, scholars over the years have searched diligently in the Scriptures for passages from the "Lost Book of Jonah." Hitzig and Renan have attributed the prophecies of Isaiah 15-23 to Jonah as being inconsistent with other parts of the book. Allusions to Moab, Egypt, and Ethiopia would certainly give Jonah a wider scope of action. He would know conditions in Tyre, Sidon, and Damascus from the Assyrian venture. Sargon's reign in Assyria (Isaiah 20:1) began in 721. It was by no means impossible that Jonah could still have been alive at the time of Isaiah.

Most scholars agree that the book of Isaiah is a compilation of at least two sources, one pre-exilic and the other composed during Judah's captivity. There is not much support for further division of the pre-exilic portion and attributing part of it to Jonah.[132]

There is something ominous in Amos's prophecy, the first part of which certainly applies to Jonah:

> ... *though they be hid from my sight in the bottom of the sea, thence will I command the serpent, and he shall bite them: and though they go into captivity before their enemies, thence will I command the sword, and it shall slay them: and I will set mine eyes upon them for evil and not for good (Amos 9:3-4).*

Muslim tradition indeed affirms that Jonah became a martyr and was buried in Nineveh. The mound of Nebi Yunus has been continuously identified with the ruins of Nineveh since early Christian times. Botta and Layard when they made separate investigations of the mound in the early 1800s were shown the tomb of the prophet. The villagers dissuaded excavation by saying, "If you disturb the tomb of the prophet he will be angry and we will suffer. Our crops will fail from lack of rain and our cattle perish from murrain."

Muslims have a preoccupation with tombs and often attach an heroic name to an obscure grave. This is most certainly true of the mosque at Nineveh shown as the tomb of Jonah. There in a richly carpeted, low-ceilinged room is a stone coffin draped in black cloth. On the wall above hangs a "tooth of the whale" which the doubter can identify as a swordfish snout. The mosque was originally a Nestorian Christian church, and the tomb is that of Mar (Saint) John the Lame. The church dates from the Caliphate when the Nestorians had a patriarch at Mosul. The tradition that Jonah was buried at Nineveh should not be completely discounted on this evidence, since there must have been some shrine connected with the prophet antedating both church and mosque.

Gath-Hepher, too, claims the tomb of its son. In Jerome's day it was two road miles from Sepphoris on the way to Tiberias. Benjamin of Tudela (12th century) states that the tomb of Jonah lay on a mountain

---

[132] Such interpreters point to the unique conjunction beginning the book of Jonah — the word *now* in Jonah 1:1 is better translated *and*.

near Sepphoris. These data point to the village of el-Meshed where the tomb is shown today in a cave.

There is another tomb shown at Bethsura near Hebron. This is consistent with the tradition that the prophet ended his service in Judah rather than Samaria. The famous mosaic map of Madaba supports this location. This map, on the floor of a church built in the sixth century, shows the area between the Dead Sea and the Mediterranean and probably originally included the area north to Asia Minor. Cities and features are not to scale, and are in only approximate locations. The tomb of Jonah is one of the few shrines shown, illustrating the importance of the prophet's life to post-exilic Jewry and early Christians.

Afterword

The author seems too modest to summarize some remarkable original conclusions. If his inferences are correct, Jonah was a state-sponsored evangelist and diplomat, acting on behalf of an official cult in Bethel. He was sent to Nineveh in Assyria to make an alliance with Apliya's rebel faction, which was friendly to Israel. In this, Jonah succeeded and changed history.

But his success in what would otherwise have been a kingdom hostile to him may have been due to the tall story he told about being rescued from the sea by a great fish. It turns out that "recovered from the water" is an even older Assyrian myth about one of their demigods, Oannes. (Unlike some scholars, Jones believes evidence that the Oannes myth predates Jonah.) The Assyrians credited Jonah's story because they had experienced the same doubly ominous portent of eclipse and earthquake that had motivated him to flee Bethel. The Ninevites were ready to accept any promise of salvation that offered hope. Oannes turns out to be the real root word for the name Jonah, and it follows that the prophet must have been named in the oral history after the Assyrian legend, not necessarily born Jonah the dove as has been thought.

The strange imagery of the gourd that sheltered Jonah loses its mystery when it is revealed that the miraculous gourd, which grew overnight, is a symbol for the protective hand of Apliya, or *apu-lilu*, "son of the night."

~~~

Don Jones was an avid student of Biblical history and archeology. Born in 1923 in Kansas City, Missouri, he was raised in a Southern Baptist household where Bible study was a daily practice. He received a Bachelor of Science in Chemical Engineering from the University of Michigan in 1942. He enlisted in the U.S. Navy and trained at the midshipman's candidate school at Notre Dame. He served out the duration of World War II as a Lieutenant Junior Grade engineering officer on an LST transport ship carrying combat troops to the Pacific theatre. After the war, he remained on Gen. MacArthur's staff in the occupation force in Japan, where he applied his knowledge of manufacturing to survey war-materiel factories and recommend ways to repurpose their output for civilian consumer products. In 1947 he was hired by Standard Oil (Indiana) and worked in the process-control lab at the Sugar Creek, Missouri refinery, which produced gasoline and aircraft fuel. In 1960, he accepted a transfer to company headquarters in Chicago, where he was a manager of petrochemical manufacturing. In 1963, he accepted a transfer to manage the company's asphalt refinery in Baltimore. Then in 1967, he accepted a another transfer to the New York headquarters of Amoco International Oil Company, followed by assignment in 1972 to the London office of Amoco Europe, where he became Vice President of Manufacturing and Marketing. In this post, he traveled extensively to visit company holdings all over the world, including a fertilizer plant in India, copper mines in Zaire, gasoline marketing in Italy, a professional conference in the Soviet Union, and business ventures in Japan and Australia.

During his time in London, one of his major projects was contracting for the building of the Milford Haven refinery and supertanker terminal in Wales, which was needed to process newly discovered crude oil from drilling rigs in the North Sea. He also represented Amoco in negotiations to comply with the nationalization of its holdings in Iran, including sale of the tanker terminal at Kharg Island in the Persian Gulf. Jones moved back to Chicago in 1979 when he joined Amoco top management as a corporate vice president. He retired in 1982 and occupied himself with family genealogical research, teaching Sunday School, and counseling small-business entrepreneurs in the SBA's Service Corps of Retired Executives (SCORE) program.

The background research and writing of this book spanned roughly a 15-year period beginning in the late 1960s. During his travels for Amoco, Jones was able visit several of the Middle Eastern locations he describes. He told the story that, when traveling in Syria, he hired a local driver to take him to various locations of interest along the coast. The driver readily agreed, but first made an unscheduled stop at a military command tent. There Jones was questioned about what business he had inspecting sites that were close to missile emplacements. Apparently he was allowed to continue, and many of his descriptions are clearly informed by his eyewitness impressions.

When living in London, he frequented the British Museum, where he was able to study its extensive collection of Middle Eastern antiquities, including Assyrian cuneiform tablets and bas reliefs. On a trip to Tehran, he stopped off in Paris to visit the Louvre. He was eager to find the statuette of Ishtar he describes, and he had a picture of it from one of his reference sources. After Jones had spent a long day fruitlessly exploring the museum's labyrinthine corridors, a friendly guard explained with the characteristic Gallic shrug that not all of the museum's holdings are on display and the desired figurine was most probably in storage.

Jones professed no knowledge of Hebrew other than the distinctions he found in Bible concordances and *The Interpreter's Bible*. As the reader will glean from his footnotes, he relies mainly on secondary sources, although for the most part these are reputable translators and scholars of long standing.

We have his manuscript in typescript, with handwritten corrections and annotations. There is no bibliography. Several of the quotations have no references or are incomplete. By searching online for key phrases, we have been able to locate most of the sources. However, the editions we cite may be not the same ones the author consulted, and we wish to correct any errors in future printings.

The reader will also note how much Jones's original inferences are informed by his unique combination of talents and background, including manufacturing (operations at Gath-Hepher and Gibeon); naval experience (seafaring, navigation, and marine biology); Middle Eastern travels (geography and archaeology); and lifelong Bible scholarship.

Even though Jones was convinced that his book offered many original and valid insights, he was apparently reluctant to publish. He feared his lack of formal academic credentials might discourage serious scholars from giving his theories careful consideration.

But despite any lack of rigor, *Searching for Jonah* offers a fresh, eclectic, and indisputably imaginative approach to interpreting one of the most famous stories in all of literature.

~~~

About the Cover Artist

Keith A. Tucker is a painter, sculptor, and designer from Nashville, Tennessee. After spending many years in New York City and learning to paint, he has created numerous pieces for stage shows and events in Las Vegas, cruise ships, libraries, and the theater. Besides *Jonah and the Whale*, his religious-themed paintings include *Baptism, Last Supper, Jesus and the Samaritan Woman* (commissioned by the United Methodist Southeastern Conference), Houston Ceiling Painting (after the style of Michelangelo's Sistine Chapel frescoes), *Triptych Icon* (for the St. Stephen Catholic Community), and *The Blessing Redeemer* (for Holy Cross Anglican Church). Many of these, as well as other commissioned and original works, can be viewed at **www.KeithTuckerArt.com.**

Appendix: Maps

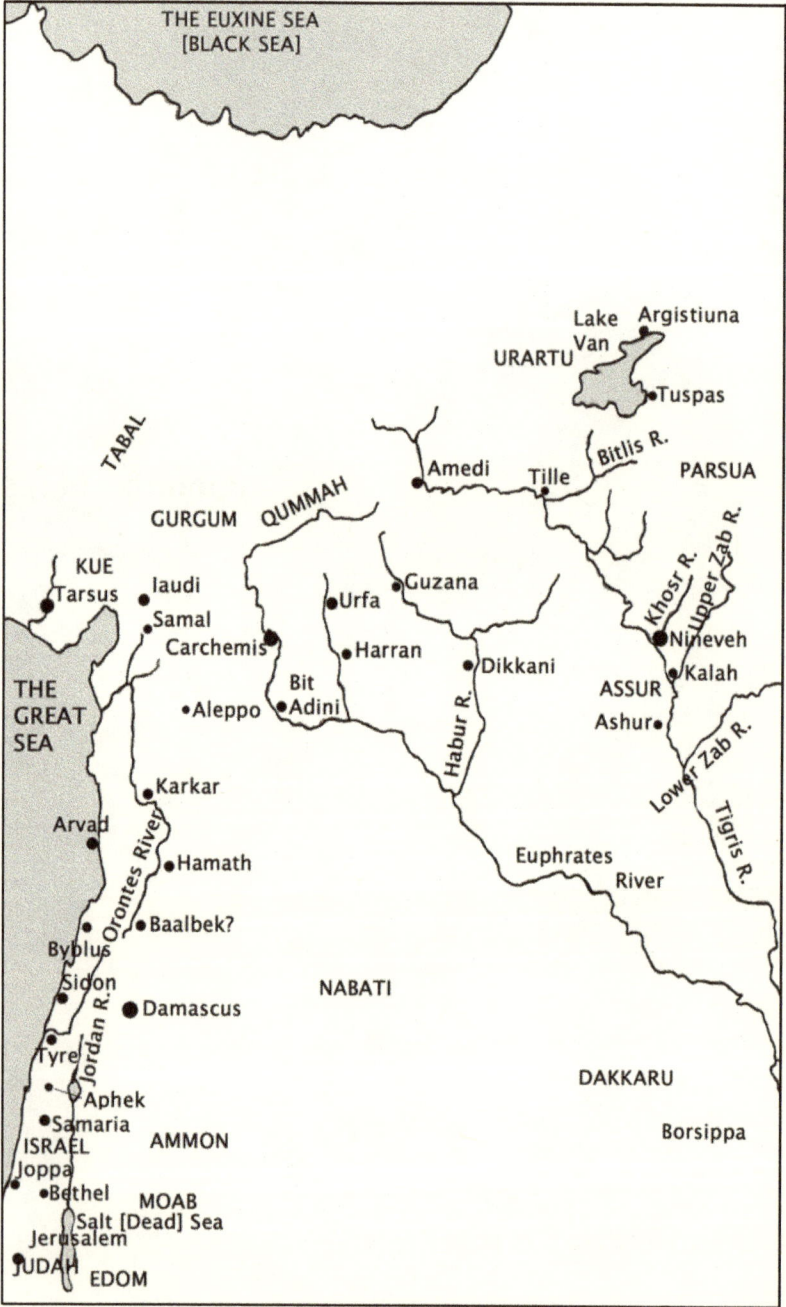

THE EUXINE SEA
[BLACK SEA]

Lake Argistiuna
URARTU Van
              •Tuspas

TABAL

Amedi   Tille   Bitlis R.   PARSUA

GURGUM QUMMAH

KUE   •Guzana
Tarsus   Iaudi   Khosr R.   Upper Zab R.
         Samal   •Urfa   •Nineveh
THE   Carchemis •Harran   •Kalah
GREAT   Bit   •Dikkani   ASSUR
SEA   •Aleppo •Adini   Ashur•
                               Habur R.   Lower Zab R.
        •Karkar   Tigris R.
Arvad
        •Hamath   Euphrates
                               River
        •Baalbek?
Byblus
Sidon   NABATI
        •Damascus

Tyre
   Aphek
•Samaria   AMMON   DAKKARU
ISRAEL
Joppa   Borsippa
  •Bethel   MOAB
         Salt [Dead] Sea
Jerusalem
JUDAH EDOM

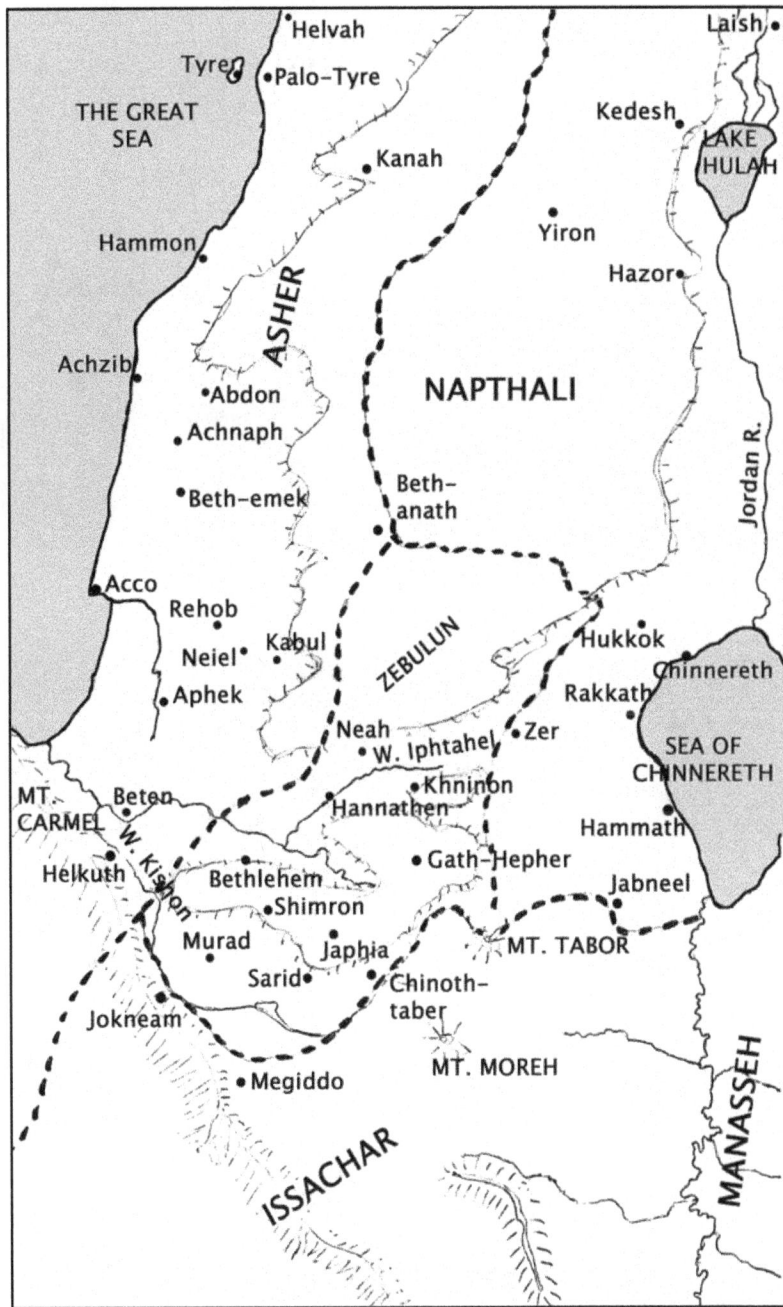

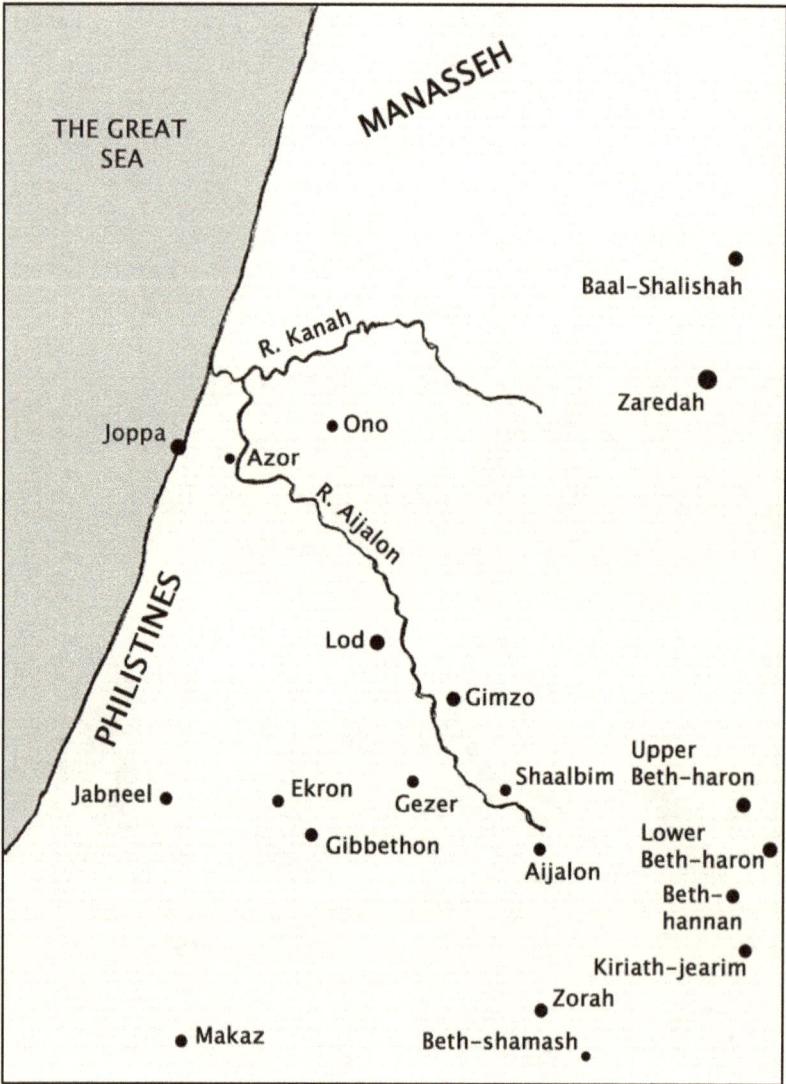

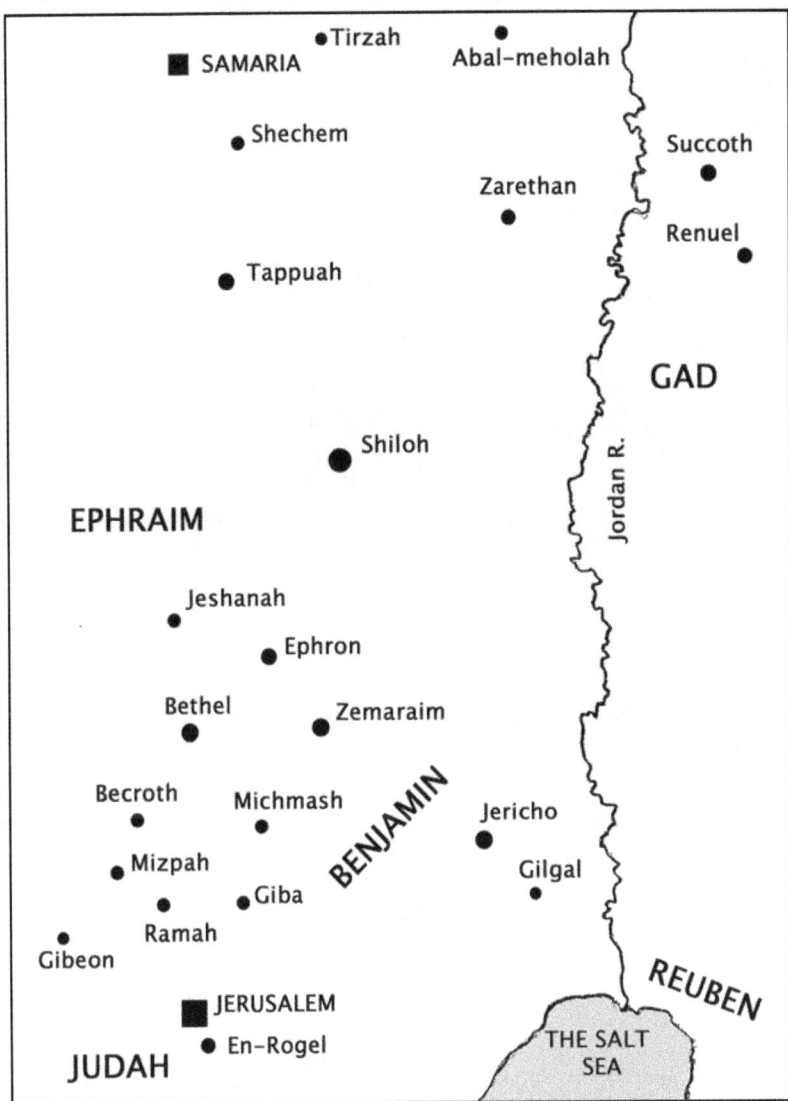

Index